IT'S UP TO US
To Fulfill the Righteousness of God

Madlyn Trone Richard

Published And Distributed By
Professional Publishing House, LLC
1425 W. Manchester Ave. Ste. B
Los Angeles, California 90047
323-750-3592
Email: professionalpublishinghouse@yahoo.com
www.Professionalpublishinghouse.com

Cover design: Mary A. Hannon
Editor: Mary A. Hannon
First printing September 2017
978-0-9983089-6-8
10 9 8 7 6 5 4 3 2 1

Table of Contents

Preface

&

THIS BOOK IS THE OUTGROWTH of a solemn conviction that I have shared with my family and sisters and brothers who follow the Lord Jesus' teachings and accept them as truth. To get the most from this book, take a walk with the Life of the Lord Jesus and listen to the words spoken by Him to John, "It's Up to Us". It is our responsibility to fulfill all righteousness, all the requirements put forth by God (Matthew 3: 15, 1). Believe the book, the Bible whose author is God. In this Book is the New Testament scripture, the veritable Word of God and His last revelation to this sin-cursed world. My book stands and rests on the fact that "It's Up to Us. " Individually, we belong to the living God. I believe with all my heart that these scriptures contain nothing but "living matter" and are as true today, and as applicable to man's needs, as they ever were. God stands ready to verify in this Book all the promises He has given the world and His people. We must do God's Will. God is the author of the Bible, His Word and His teaching. In church I observe ministers and preachers discussing everything but Scripture. When they tell their stories the Lord Jesus is either mentioned once in a while or compared to someone or left out (Hebrews 3:4; 12). He who built all things is God. These words are added to refer to the house of which Jesus is the builder and the owner. God is its ultimate author and Jesus Christ is the builder and proprietor of the institution of Christianity. All of this is done by the Son under the appointment of the Father. Please be advised that in writing this book I don't claim absolute perfection. There is much improvement that can be made that the intelligent reader will not fail to recognize. I am following God's system (John 17:17). Teach the truth, ministers, teach your audience the truth by giving them a correct understanding of His Word and His Word is truth. The Bible is the Word of God and it contains His system of purification, the Gospel of Jesus in its fullest meaning with all its provisions for the wants of our sinful race. In writing this book, my one aim is to bring out and share as much as I am able, the truth about Jesus. Some people asked if I might be afraid that my plain translation will injure the sale of this book. Not at all, not in the least. Money has nothing to do with it. A billion dollars cannot change God's Word, His Son Jesus' teaching and the teaching of John the Baptist. God's Word is truth. In Revelations 22:18 we are told not to change God's Word. If anyone shall add or take away from God's Word they will meet a dreadful doom such as the plagues that are written in His Book. The Bible is in the beginning and is God's Word, His system and His guide. He was in the beginning and will be in the ending. Some intellectuals, ministers, teachers and religious folk say the Bible was about back then but what do they mean? The Word was in the beginning and it has not changed. If God changes what is going to happen to us? We are His children and we were made in His likeness. The Lord God and His Son Jesus are in us and for us. Accept His Son Jesus and cast your burdens on the Lord and He shall sustain you and never permit the Righteous to be moved. (Psalms 55:22)

(Romans 8:31). God is for us (Col 2:8). Don't let anyone rob you with their philosophy. It is not good for any person, minister, teacher or religious leader to teach their own doctrine and not Jesus' teaching. (Matthew 9:13) Jesus' teaching is that He desires mercy and not sacrifice (Hosea 6:6). This means that God prizes a merciful disposition by deeds of kindness and mercy far more than the performance of outward rites and ceremonies. Jesus said that He did not come to call the righteous but sinners. The forgiveness of sins and healing of diseases are of God. (Matthew 7:21) Do God's Will, not by your words or professions but by His requirement, the Bible. The same Bible that teaches the wrath, anger and judgment of God also teaches the love, mercy and long suffering of God. All biblical literature is based on the Word and the findings when the Bible was first written. No one wants to accept the King James version but for the last 2000+ years millions and millions of Bibles have been written based on information from the King James version. With many changes and hundreds of different names, where did they get their material from? King James was the original Bible and God is the author (Psalms 103:1;19, 9) . Read the Bible because the Word is truth (Hebrews 7:26). Jesus is separate from sinners. Study God's Word.

TRAVEL WITH ME

In this book of righteousness you have a wonderful treat in store. Travel with me and may God bless you as you begin to live in its pages. God Jesus is not an after-thought, He is Our Leader, Our Father, Our Life, and Our Health. He owns the world and everything in it. He is truly Our Father so don't come dragging Him into your life later (John 4:24). God is Spirit and we must worship Him through Jesus His Son, in spirit and truth. In our worship services He should be in charge, the Holy Spirit. Remember He is not an after-thought (Revelations 19:10). Don't worship any one person (Revelations 3:21). Follow Jesus in all things.

GENERATIONS

All generations leading up to Jesus are fourteen. There were certain omissions which the Jews probably understood which made in all, forty-two generations in round numbers from Abraham to Jesus. Jacob was Joseph's father, the husband of Mary (Matthew 1:16).

The Birth of Jesus (Matthew 1:18) Mary, having been espoused to Joseph and engaged to be married, was found to be with child of the Holy Spirit. Humanity of Jesus (Hebrews 10:5), (Luke1:35) Not wishing to expose her to shame Joseph, Mary's husband, a righteous man, was thinking about these things when an angel of the Lord appeared to him in a dream and told him not to fear but to take Mary as his wife. The child within her is of the Holy Spirit and she will bring forth a son and you shall call his name Jesus and he shall save his peoples from themselves and from the pollution of power, guilt, and the penalty of all sin. Jesus was born a Jew in Bethlehem of Judea rather than in Bethlehem of Galilee. (Matthew 2:1-23) There was a king named Herod who was an Edomite, a Jewish man of great wickedness and cruelty. According to tradition, King Herod believed that there would be born in Judea one who would hold universal dominion and he was afraid. A star was seen in the East and there is no doubt that this star was divinely appointed to guide the Wise Men to the place where they learned that the infant was born. King Herod was troubled, he feared a rival and his fear spread among the people of his realm. Privately, he asked the Wise Men exactly where the star appeared and sent them to Bethlehem to inquire about the Baby Child, find him and bring back word so that Herod could worship him. This crafty king had no notion of worshiping the Child but meant to kill him. The Wise Men went from Jerusalem to Bethlehem with the star guiding their way and the star stood over the very spot where the Child was. The Wise Men had been warned in a dream not to return to Herod. In all ages, God has given warning to His people in a dream or vision. God would not suffer these Wise Men to aid Herod in his wicked purpose. An angel of God appeared to Joseph in a dream to take the Child and his mother and flee to Egypt. It is perfectly easy for the all wise God to obstruct all human schemes and disrupt the plans of the Devil. (Matthew 2) Herod was an enraged monster who slew all male children from two years and younger. After Herod died an angel of the Lord appeared to Joseph in a dream in Egypt and told him to take the mother and Child into the land of Israel. Obeying the Lord, Joseph learned that Herod's son was over Judea and he feared to go there. Warned in a dream, he went into a part of Galilee, a city called Nazareth which was a town very much despised. It was said that a Nazarene was exceedingly hated (Isaiah 53: 2;3). Joseph obeyed God, listened and heard what the Lord was directing him to do. Call his name Jesus and He will save his people from the pollution, power, guilt and penalty of sin. This was a proper name for Jesus because He is God manifested in the flesh.

TWELVE YEARS OLD

Jesus is twelve years old and according to custom, every year his folks traveled to the Feast of the Passover in Jerusalem. They were returning home and had traveled one day before realizing he wasn't in the crowd. They spent three days looking for him and found him in the Temple asking the teachers questions. His parents were amazed and his mother asked him, "Child, why do you treat us this way?" He asked them why they were looking for him because he was occupied with his Father's matters and was taking care of his Father's business. He returned with them to Nazareth and respectfully worked with his father Joseph, a carpenter, until he was 30 years old. (Luke 2).

Baptizing and immersed in the Jordon River, John is preaching repentance. He is preaching about giving up your sins. John the Baptist challenges the Pharisees and Saducees not to try and take the easy way out, a way that is saturated with insincerity, righteous deeds and fruit worthy of repentance. Show that I feel so righteous by knowing the Lord Jesus' reality of your repentance by forsaking sin in every form (Matt 3:15)

John, seeing Jesus coming from Galilee to Jordon to be immersed by him, felt a great inferiority to Jesus and shrank from the idea of immersing him. John felt the need to be immersed by Jesus. But Jesus answered, "It becomes us to fulfill all righteousness, all the requirements of God. "

My faith is in the Lord and this book is based upon the statements that Jesus is speaking. It is up to us and to Jesus and John to fulfill all righteousness that is a requirement of God. I feel righteous by knowing the Lord Jesus and studying His teaching, training and preaching. All of His work is and was God's, His Father's Will. I ask the Lord Jesus to teach me how to do His Will and keep me humble.

PALESTINE IN THE TIME OF JESUS

Jesus was about thirty years old and living in Palestine when the time was ripe for him to begin his teaching and ministry that would take him, the Savior of Mankind, to the cross on Calvary, the last scene in the great tragedy that was to change the religious faith of an entire world. As a rule, little attention is given to the prevailing conditions at that time. In Sunday school class one often hears the question: What was it like then? Will this story shine some light upon this subject? I hope so.

With all of the changes that man has made in nations, including maps redrawn, countries renamed, things added and deleted, Palestine, then as now, remains situated on the eastern shores of the Mediterranean. It was so hot in summer that men were forced to wear only the thinnest and loosest of clothing while winters were characterized by cold winds and rains that often swelled the land's narrow streams into raging torrents. Rarely, however, was ice or snow seen except on the tops of mountains. The southern end of the land was bare and rocky, dwindling off into a desert. To the north, the country was richer while in the section around Nazareth, where Jesus spent his youth and early manhood, it was full of green and fertile valleys. In this region where nature smiled, there grew oranges, lemons, olives, dates, grapes, apples, wheat, barley, almonds, and many other delicious fruits, vegetables and grains. Flowers and plants such as the daisy, poppy, marigold, Rose of Sharon, lily, tulip, and crocus flourished in abundance.

The tall palm, broad sycamore, cypress, myrtle, bay and oleander lent their share of shade and beauty to the landscape. Birds of the air were much the same in variety as those of similar climates while the hyena, leopard, wolf, jackal, deer and smaller varieties of animal life haunted lonely places.

In the village streets the unlovely cur, doubtless, barked then as now as strangers passed to and fro. Men hunted in the hills, fished in the Sea of Galilee, cultivated farms and gardens, tended their flocks or bartered in the towns and cities for their living. There was also a great class that earned its daily bread by working for hire in the interest of others.

Jesus had a great love of nature and we often find him speaking of the things he saw around him; flowers, birds, animals, trees, mountains, plains, valleys, water courses and living things in the waters. All of these things spread out before him in Palestine were examples of his Father's loving care in providing for mankind.

Jesus' deepest concern, however, must have been for the men and women, boys and girls who populated the land, for it was these and the ones to follow all over the world, that he had come to save. What did he find? When David was King of the Jews he ruled the entire country. God promised the land to the Jews but they did not obey Him so the Roman kings ruled the land. Roman soldiers marched in the city streets and tax collectors collected all the money they could. The Jews were allowed to practice their religion but that was all. So low was this nation that claimed to be God's only people on earth and so deeply rooted was their hope of escape from this situation that they had but one thought; when and how might they be delivered?

In earlier days the Jews became careless about their religion and drifted easily into idolatry. All desire for such worship disappeared. The opposite took root in its place and Jews became obsessed with obeying God to the smallest letter of the law. This was good had they not overlooked the most important practice, to love and have mercy for those in need.

Synagogues were formed where ten or more families assembled, read the Law and had it explained to them. In addition, once each year zealous Jews listened to the entire Old Testament and had it explained. These synagogues offered Jesus a splendid opportunity to learn and later to speak. They also opened the door for Paul to reach out to the Jewish people.

Jesus found that the Jews didn't have religion in their heart. For most it was an outward appearance and only a few men and women were truly devout. During four hundred years the voice of a prophet had not been heard and the pure speaking stream of truth had become dark and murky with error and formality. The Pharisees were religious people of the day and their purpose was distinct and apart from the world around them. This was a very good idea in itself that Jesus commanded but he wished it to be carried out in a different manner. The Pharisees were leaders of worship and they professed to be well versed in the Law, the prophets and especially the tradition of the elders. They knew the Old Testament down to the words and letters but they never caught the heart of the Word and Jesus was very plain in telling them so. The Sadducees stood against this form of religion. They were of the wealthier class and for the most part, gave themselves over to social pleasure. Below these two classes were the common people, many of whom longed for a shepherd but had none. Those who should have been leaders were blind themselves, seeking to consume and not to save. Looking back, they could point to patriarchs of greatest piety, kings after God's own heart, prophets speaking fiery messages against sin in their day, psalmists who sang the true songs of Zion, all towering high in lives of faith and hope but that was all in the past. Jesus found no such faith, no such loyalty and no sincere worship. There was no response to his higher and better life except from confessions of sinners with whom the Jews wouldn't mingle. Despite the fact that every Jew was looking for the promised Messiah, when He did come they rejected his teaching, said he had a devil, and finally hated him and his words so much that they nailed him to a tree/cross to get rid of him. Yet that cross and the resurrection that followed is the hope of every child of God today.

It should be strongly impressed upon every child in Sunday school or Christian education classes that the study of the times and conditions in which Jesus lived is necessary for a thorough understanding of the lessons. Books and maps are available on these subjects and they should be studied by teachers and communicated to the children. Children should also read these books and have discussions with their teachers. These are good methods of instilling into young minds valuable information concerning Judea, the Jews, Jewish history and the manners and customs that prevailed at the time Jesus went to Calvary to pay for mankind's sin.

A PRINCIPLE

To fulfill all righteousness is a version of the Gospel. In fact, Jesus sustains a demand for a higher righteousness than that practiced by the

Jewish religious establishment of the time. Both the Greek and Hebrew term for righteousness also means justice.

Remember, Jesus was born into Judaism. He traveled throughout Galilee teaching in the Jewish synagogues. In Biblical times the synagogue was not thought of as a sacred space to worship. The word is a Greek term that meant assembly or gathering that could be held any place where people gathered for studying God's Word or to take care of religious affairs of the community. The institution of the synagogue seems to have emerged as a survival technique during the 6th century B. C. as part of the distinctive religion that came to be called Judaism.

Jesus went throughout Galilee preaching the Gospel and healing every disease in the Jewish synagogues. Jesus still heals those who obey and trust Him (Matt 4:23). People were under the control of demons until Jesus came to drive them out and infuse His own life into them (Luke 21:22). All diseases can be healed by the Great Physician and healing is part of the Gospel that will last through the Gospel dispensation.

Keep in mind, after Jesus was immersed by John, the Spirit led Him into the wilderness to be tempted by the Devil. All those who receive the Holy Spirit are going to be tried, tempted or tested by the Devil. Remember Adam and Eve and the snake. Eve was tempted along the same lines as Jesus and she fell (John 1:2;16). Satan would have led Jesus to work a miracle to satisfy his own hunger but Jesus refused. It has been written, "Obedience to God's Word in all things is the surest way of having all our needs supplied." (Phillipians 4:19).

CALLED

Jesus called twelve Disciples. In studying God's Word, I find the number twelve has a lot to do with God's people (Revelations 21) (Matthew 10).

PETER, whose name means "rock", was brought to Jesus by his brother. He soon became a leader of the disciples and was the first to say that Jesus was the Son of God.

ANDREW and his brother were fishing when Jesus said to them, "Follow me, and I will make you fishers of men." From that day on, Andrew served Jesus.

JAMES, the son of Zebedee, was a fisherman. He was one of the three disciples closest to Jesus and was the first disciple to die for Him.

JOHN was called by Jesus to give up fishing and follow Him. He was very close to Jesus and was called the "beloved" disciple. John wrote the book of Revelations.

PHILIP was so happy when he found Jesus that he ran to tell his friend Nathanael about Him. Philip became one of the disciples who saw Jesus do many wonderful things.

BARTHOLOMEW first heard about Jesus from Philip. He did not believe that Jesus was the Son of God until he had seen him and talked with him.

THOMAS was a brave disciple. He is called "the doubter" because at first he would not believe when the other disciples said they had seen Jesus after the Resurrection.

MATTHEW was a tax collector who left his work to follow Jesus. He is the author of the book in the Bible called "St. Matthew".

JAMES, the son of Alpheus, was one of the apostles who spent his time preaching and witnessing for Jesus.

THADDAEUS was one of the twelve that Jesus sent forth to preach. He was the brother of James and was sometimes called Judas.

SIMON was a member of a Jewish group of people called Canaanites who were much hated. He was chosen as one of the disciples and served Jesus the rest of his life.

JUDAS ISCARIOT was the disciple who handled the money for the group. One day Judas betrayed Jesus for thirty pieces of silver. Judas felt bad because of what he had done and went out and hanged himself.

Jesus called these twelve disciples to Himself. They were twelve apostles, men not women, who were called and later sent with full equipment for service that came from Jesus. These men were the highest officials close to Jesus and were given the responsibility of doing His will. Jesus gave them the authority over unclean spirits that were under the control of demons until Jesus drove them out and then infused His own life within them (Luke 11:21;22). He healed those who were afflicted because all diseases can be healed by the Great Physician. Healing is part of the Gospel and it appears throughout the Gospel. Jesus also gave the Disciples authority over unclean spirits and demonstrated that all unclean spirits are under His control. After casting them out He healed the afflicted. The full equipment for healing comes from Jesus (Matthew10:5). Jesus sent forth the Twelve telling them not to go the way of the Gentiles or Samaritans who were a combination of Jews and Pagans. These people occupied the country formerly belonging to Ephraim and the half-tribe of Manasseh, the lost sheep of the House of Israel. The tribes of Judah and Benjamin represented the bulk of the Israelites who returned from the Babylonian captivity. There were people of other tribes intermixed with those mentioned and these were the only representatives of the House of Israel in Palestine. The Gospel was first preached to all of these people (Peter 1:2). God always knew all that would occur in the world and His choosing of people for salvation was according to His foreknowledge.

Two Historical Writers Of The New Testament Matthew and John

The historical books of the New Testament differ from those of the Old Testament in that they tell of the life of Jesus and the spread of the faith. Jesus was born into Judaism but his teaching was not accepted by the Jews.

The first three of the four Gospels are called synoptical gospels, because they give a synopsis, or general view, of Christ's life. The fourth Gospel, that of John, is called the doctrinal Gospel, because it teaches specifically the doctrine of the divine nature of Christ as the Son of God. Four different points of view are expressed in the Gospels and to each of them interpreters of Scripture have assigned a symbol, based upon Ezekiel 1:4-10. The Acts has often been called the Gospel of the Holy Spirit.

John the Immerser. The Immerser is a title given to John because he immersed people in the wilderness of Judea. It borders the Jordan and the Dead Sea and is a country used for pasturage. (Matthew 3;1).

Matthew was the Gospel written for the Jews. It shows Jesus as the Messiah and King in whom all the great Old Testament prophecies were fulfilled. Matthew was a Jew and a man of humble birth. His Gospel was written about 60 A. D. Its symbol is a man and it has twenty-eight chapters.

John was the Gospel that may be said to have been directed to all mankind. John was the youngest of the apostles and has been honored with the title "the disciple whom Jesus loved. " His Gospel is probably the greatest of all. It was written later than the others (probably about the year 85 A. D.) and dwells upon Jesus as the Lord and Word Made Flesh. Its symbol is an eagle and it contains twenty-one chapters.

QUESTIONS AND ANSWERS ABOUT THE GOSPELS

What a reward and happiness I find in studying the life and teaching-preaching of Jesus. I have found wisdom and I pray to gain understanding as I write.

THE FOUR GOSPELS

1. What are the names of the four Gospels? Matthew, Mark, Luke, and John.

2. What is the subject of these four books? The life and ministry of Jesus Christ.

3. Who was the Evangelist Matthew? He was a publican who became one of the Twelve Apostles.

4. What are the characteristics of Matthews Gospels? Matthew wrote for the Jews to prove Jesus was the Messiah.

5. Who was the Evangelist Mark? Mark was one of those who believed in Jesus during His life and became prominent in the Church.

6. What are the characteristics of Mark's Gospel? Mark's Gospel was the earliest Christian writing and seems to have been written specifically for the Gentile Christians. He omits a considerable part of Jesus' life. He begins with the ministry of John and writes about what he learned from those who saw and heard Jesus' teaching.

7. Who was the Evangelist Luke? Luke was a Greek physician said to have been born in Antioch, Syria. He was a great friend of the Apostle Paul and also wrote the Acts, partly from his own experiences.

8. What are the characteristics of Luke's Gospel? Luke is the only Gospel that describes the infancy of Jesus. In many places he shows the influence of his medical training and it is very historically accurate. Luke does not profess to write as an eye witness but one who carefully collected his material from who were. (Acts1:1;4). He has much in common with Matthew's Gospel because it was written for the Jews. Luke seems to have been writing for the whole world

but more for the Gentiles. (Luke 4:25;27) (Luke 9:51;56) . He was the one who took it in hand to put in order the facts that had been confirmed. God selected his own men to give the New Testament scriptures to the world. He used them for that purpose.

9. The ministry of John the Baptist. (Matthew 3: 1;2) (Mark1: 1;8) (Luke 3:1;18) Who was Tiberius? The second Emperor of Rome.

10. Who was John the Baptist? The forerunner sent to prepare the way for Jesus.

11. What prophecy had been spoken concerning him? "Behold, I will send you Elijah the Prophet before the coming of the great and dreadful day of the Lord and he shall turn the heart of the fathers to the children, and the heart of the children to the fathers, lest I come and smite with a curse." (Mal 4:5;6).

12. What were the special features of John's preaching? John preached about repentance and forgiveness of sin through the coming of the Lord Jesus, the Messiah. Baptism is the outward sign of this repentance.

13. What is repentance? Repentance is a sorrow for sin that produces a change in mind and heart.

14. Was John's preaching successful? Yes, people from all parts of Judea confessed their sins and were baptized. (Matt3:5;6) (Mark 1:5;7).

15. What special merit did John recommend to those who came to him? John recommended generosity, honesty, kindness and contentment.

16. What is the fruit of true repentance? Ceasing to do evil willfully and habitually (Isa 1:16).

17. Who were the Publicans? The Publicans were Jewish collectors of Roman taxes.

18. Why were the Publicans so odious and hateful to their countrymen? Although they were Jews who aided their Roman masters who oppressed them, some were dishonest and worked for their own gain.

19. What is the meaning of the word "Christ"? Christ means Anointed One (Luke 4:18).

20. What was the difference between John's baptism and Our Lord's baptism? John's baptism was the baptism of repentance, the symbol of a desire to live a new life that should show the fruit of repentance. Our Lord's was the baptism of the Holy Spirit.

21. What is the meaning of Baptism with Fire? Baptism with Fire means the purifying force of the Holy Spirit (Corinthians 1:3;13).

FASCINATED WITH THE WORD

Searching and reading about the beginning of creation one finds out that the Word is God. This asserts the essential deity of Jesus whose divinity has existed from eternity. A word is a sign or representation of an idea or of a fact. Jesus, the Word, is an expression of the Father's thought of mercy for our sinful race (John 1-14). And the Word became flesh and lived among us, putting on a human body and becoming a human being (Isa 9: 6). He was before me because He existed from all eternity and all things were made through Him. All things outside of God Himself must trace their being or existence to Him (Hebrews 1: 2). In Him is life and He is the source of all natural and spiritual life. Angels, men and all animate existence springs from Him. Jesus is our spiritual life (John 14: 6; 3, 4). John's Gospel has much more to say about the divinity of Jesus than the other three Evangelists. John was one of the three Apostles who made up Jesus' Cabinet, Peter and James being the other two. These three witnessed many miracles (Mark 5:37), (Matt 17: 1), (Matt 26: 37). John was called the disciple that Jesus loved. John's Gospel has comparatively little in common with the other Gospels. It seems that Matthew, Mark and Luke were more concerned about Jesus' ministry around Galilee. In John's Gospel the chief characteristic that we see is that he gives a much fuller account of Jesus unfolding as His own Divine Person with the indwelling of the Spirit. In other words, John dwells more on the knowledge of God. The other Evangelists deal with the objective knowledge of Him. This difference is radical because it has to do with the development of the very overworked word Christian and Christian character. John was about the more abundant life (John 1:31), (Peter 2:24; 3, 18), (Galatians 3:13). Jesus expiated human guilt by His own vicarious death on the cross. He bore our sins in His own body on the tree. The sins of all were laid on Jesus (Isa. 53:6) and He put them away by the sacrifice of Himself (Hebrews 9:12; 8, 26). Good things are to come with the Gospel and these things are typified in the mosaic economy. A greater and more perfect Tabernacle is Heaven itself, where Jesus represents His people.

To Fulfill All Righteousness

All my life, when I was growing up and going to Church, I've been fascinated with the stories and the teachings of Jesus, God and His Government. I listened to my folks talk about Church in a positive way, I attended Sunday School and later became a Sunday School teacher. During this time I came to understand that knowledge without obedience amounts to nothing (Romans 2; 17-23). I also learned that a willingness to do the will of God is one of the best preparations for receiving a knowledge of His Will (John:7;17).

The Crucified Jesus

The Crucified Jesus was the central theme in the Apostles' preaching (Corinthians 1:2;2). Paul had to be knocked down and blinded on the road to Damascus and he heard God's and Jesus' voice asking why he was persecuting Him. We are doing it today by not doing God's Will and the Will of the Lord Jesus. The Bible, the Word of God, is truth. He gave us His Only Begotten Son who was becoming one of us and was needed by us (Hebrews 7:26). Such a One alone could meet our needs and was made higher than the heavens.

Jesus was called to do God's Will, not his own will. Paul was called by the Lord Jesus to the office of an Apostle (Acts 18:17 with its accompaniments). Paul preached and taught God's word. He didn't joke about it, change it to suit his or his followers feelings but he taught the truth. His preaching and teaching relates to spiritual character or Christ-likeness. One does not begin to live successfully according to the Scriptures until he has thought about filling the spirit of Jesus in his heart and putting the government of his on his shoulder.

Paul's teaching is not from man or through man (Galatians1:25) Why don't Christians, or those professed to be Christians, like Paul's teaching or preaching? It is the truth. Paul didn't set aside the grace of God as if it was of no value like the false teachers, preachers and ministers are doing today. They deliver their message and act as if righteousness is through the law. If there is any other way of salvation than through Jesus, His death was needless.

ELDER

I served as an ordained Elder of the Pasadena Presbyterian Church for nine years. After serving for three years, I took one year off, and then went back on session for nine years.

For two years during that time I served as Clerk of Session for Reverend Vahe H. Simonian, with the Lord Jesus watching over me. I could not have done this alone, even though I had good tutoring and training from Elder John Norquest who had been a Clerk for the Presbyterian Church for thirty years. Pastor Simonian had our Church at heart. He was a very dynamic speaker and after he left no speaker has been as clear and outspoken as he was.

As I think about this time I remember the pleasure of working with my Christian sisters and brothers who were elders on session with me and who respected me as their Clerk for two years of that session. I remember the worth of character, the influence of example, the dignity of simplicity, the power of kindness, the success of perseverance, the wisdom of economy, the joy of originating and the profit of experience. Remembering only what we do for Christ will last. I walk by the Spirit, under His guidance and influence, not fulfilling the desires of the flesh (Galatians 16:17).

Plain Truth

"If you are the Christ, tell us plainly." It must have been a wag who quipped, in a moment of pique, that every profession is a conspiracy against the non-professional, that is, against lay people like ourselves.

For instance, you take lawyers. They forever keep us dependent upon them by embalming the law in what we might call "legalese." Now "legalese" is a mixture of ancient English and encrusted Latin, and every time they throw it at us we say, "Surely we are dependent upon them because we don't know what they're talking about," but surely they do.

Doctors also do this to us. They keep us in our place by long and technical words which describe our ailments. It we were not ill before we went to visit them, after they finish describing our condition, we surely are ill thereafter.

We have found this to be very true in the fields of technology and science. Scientists always keep us at bay, because they resort to symbols and language which only the initiate can understand. It's a closed little corporation. They know the language which is thrown around—I think—but surely we don't.

Has this not been true of ministers and the church in general? We deliberately try to confound the simple verities of the gospel such as faith, hope and love, with all of the confusing languages of theology, ancient languages, Greek words and Hebrew sayings that are far beyond our comprehension, as well as the comprehension of the average minister—but he enjoys throwing them out anyway.

Now this was the kind of charge which was levied against Jesus in the scene which we read to you this morning. It's wintertime. It's cold. The followers of Jesus are seeking some shelter. They have come into the Temple. They are trying to gain that shelter at Solomon's porch. The Feast of Dedication is taking place at this time in the Jewish calendar, so there are many Jews at the Temple as well.

Suddenly Jesus is hemmed in by angry Jews. They ask: "How long will you keep us in suspense? If you are the Christ, tell us plainly."

Now this word "plainly" is one of John's favorite words. He uses it about nine times in his Gospel. The word "plainly" basically means "Without the obscurity of a parable."

Jesus, you will remember, taught in parables, and you had to be tuned in to the parable, in order to understand it. So what "plainly" means is, "Tell us without the use of a parable. Tell us openly and publicly, without trying to hide it. If you are the Christ, tell us plainly,"—those words—"that you are the Christ."

Well, the question may have been raised by these Jews to bait Jesus, to declare himself as the Christ, so that they could arrest him and put him away. Or perhaps, the request on the other hand, could have come out of a deep desire to understand who Jesus really was. Let's be generous this morning and concede that the second motive is true. Let's dismiss the first one.

Regardless of which motive—Jesus would not oblige. He would not tell them that he was the Christ plainly. You know the lack of communication is not only due to the inability to tell something; it is also due to the inability to hear something.

There is no time in the Gospel records that I can see that Jesus came out boldly and said, "I am the Christ," at certain times in his ministry because he felt that it might lead to his crucifixion prematurely. Or on the other hand he might have felt that this term "Christ" or "Messiah" might easily be misunderstood by those who would hear him. The term meant different things to different people during Jesus' time, and therefore he never came out and said, "I am the Christ."

On the other hand, we find that Jesus did refer to himself as "the bread of life," as "the water of life," as "the son of man," "the good shepherd," "the light of the world." These were terms that he addressed to himself.

He did mighty works throughout Galilee and Judea. He forgave people their sins. Therefore the question is rightfully asked, when seeing all of these various things happening, "If you are the Christ, you call yourself all these names. This is what you are doing. If you are the Christ, tell us plainly."

Apparently it has been plain enough for some folk—the sheep in the pasture—it was plain enough for James and John. It was plain enough for Peter and Andrew. It was plain enough for Mary of Magdala. It was plain enough for the demoniac of Gadara, for Zacchaeus, for Mary and Martha of Bethany and a host of others. It was plain enough for them.

So it depended upon the communication of the listener, as well as the one who was to give the communication itself.

Communication is not achieved by clarity alone. It amazes me how, at the conclusion of a morning worship service like this, most of you listen to the sermon attentively. Then we go into the Gamble lounge, and if I were to ask you to tell me what you heard, your replies would be amazing. Sometimes I have to wonder if you have been here this morning and perhaps the communication is my problem but quite often it is also your problem. That is, the hearer has a problem in communication, as well as the speaker.

One's affinity for truth is in the picture of communication. We come to truth with a mind-set. We come with a mind-set that either we are going to receive what we are going to hear, or we are going to reject what we are going to hear, or we are going to criticize what we are going to hear or we are going to find something wrong with what we are going to hear. Therefore, with a mind-set we can't. That filter we call the brain, as the communication goes out and is filtered through to your own experience, can end up something totally different from what the communicator had intended.

Jesus, for example, spoke in parables—veiled truth—and those who wished to hear what he had to say heard it; those who had a disposition not to hear what he had to say, didn't hear it. But they both listened to the parable.

Notice, for instance, the eighth chapter of Luke in describing the phenomenon: "To you it has been given to know the secret of the Kingdom of God; but for others they are in parables, so that seeing they may not see, and hearing they do not understand." That's found in Luke 8:10, if you want to look it up when you go home.

What I am suggesting is that if you want to understand a communication, then you have to at least meet truth part way. You have to come with a readiness, an expectation and imagination and a willingness to participate in the truth. What we suffer in society is a lack of imagination. We do not participate in the truth. We don't imagine it within our own existence.

W. H. Auden traced the blame of this to the advent of television. He says that in the old days of radio—and I am sure we recall those days—we had to meet the program part way; otherwise if we didn't use our imagination, there was no way to realize what was going on in radio.

For instance, when we listened to Amos and Andy over the radio, we had to have a mental image, right or wrong, of what Amos and Andy were trying to say and what they looked like. As a youngster when I turned on the radio and listened for The Lone Ranger I knew in my own mind what the Lone Ranger looked like. When he finally made television he turned out to be something else, but on radio at least I had to meet him part way.

Now when television came along, so went imagination; in fact imagination went to sleep. Only on rare occasions, perhaps in the news, do we participate in what is going on as far as truth is concerned.

Jesus is saying here that the truth about who I am has been sounded, but you have not heard. It reminds me of the tourist recently in the Pasadena Museum standing before a masterpiece saying, "I don't see anything in that." The tourist standing next to him replied, "Don't you wish you could?"

"If you are Christ, tell us plainly." Well the answer is clear: "When you are ready to hear, you will."

At this point I think that a demand has also been made upon the church and upon us as ministers—and not without justification. "If he is the Christ," you are saying to me many times, "tell us plainly."

Our times are out of joint, are they not? People today are hungry for the word. There was a time when people were not interested in what the pulpit had to say; we were interested only in being activists, not concerned about the worship service.

It's interesting that our Research Department of the General Assembly has recently come out with a survey made across the country that what persons want from their church today is to hear the word—plainly. The church needs to repent for having failed to declare the message of Jesus Christ with greater clarity. We have developed a kind of jargon which speaks only to those of us who are inside the little circle and says very little to the person who is outside.

Have you ever tried to assemble a toy on Christmas Eve in the wee hours of the morning for your children? Try it sometime. Some of you for your grandchildren. I mentioned this at the 9:30 service and one of our church members offered to come to my home next Christmas and do the assembling. Let me tell you my experience about trying to assemble toys.

We have some magnificent toys that have never been assembled. There is a note on the carton in which the toy comes which declares that a child can assemble this toy in five minutes. And that perhaps is one of the reasons why I cannot; it takes a child to assemble it.

You open up the carton and you come upon a sleazy diagram which is undoubtedly the last copy that has been coughed up by a tired A. B. Dick machine at the end of a long run. You take a look at this diagram and you say, "Tell us plainly—tell us plainly, "—hopefully you say this. And then you take a look at the instructions. They go something like this—I just took this at random amongst the many toys:

> Take crossbar A and fasten to upright C, keeping the curved edge to the lower center. Tighten the Ferguson Bolt (who in the world is Ferguson?), making sure that the lock washer is facing bar B. Insert at this time the bracing rod into opening C, making sure that the corner braces are in a 90 degree angle to tube D. Snap the end rods in place by pressing with the thumb at point A-2 and then attach the wheels as marked.

In the wee hours of Christmas Eve this is what Santa Claus has to face. Do you wonder then that the world turns to the church and says, "Look, this is the kind of game you are playing on Christmas Eve. If he is the Christ, tell us plainly—tell us plainly who he is."

And what do we come back with? Oh—we come back with eleven thick volumes of Barth's <u>Dogmatics</u>. We come back, when people ask us to tell them about Christ plainly, with Tillich's answers, three closely reasoned volumes of theology. We come back with Bultmann's answers in two volumes to New Testament Theology and a very complicated work on demythologizing—a word we can't even spell—and the world turns to us and says, "Tell us plainly." The world says, "Give us bread," and we give them a stone. They say, "Give us fish," and we hand them a scorpion.

And the ministers are to blame on the local level. We have a job of translating what the theologians are saying. We need to break the language down. We need to be able to break it down, so that you, the people, can understand what theology is all about. Unfortunately, pastors frequently are as obtuse as the theologians they read.

I remember one time when I had a wedding, the father of the bride gave me a gift. It was a book and I took off the cover and read the title of the book. It was: <u>Write Clearly, Speak Effectively</u>. I wonder how he knew—you know he had never heard me preach, and yet he gave me a book.

<u>Write Clearly and Speak Effectively.</u>

Krister Stendahl, the great New Testament scholar at Harvard Divinity School, who is now dean of the Harvard Divinity School used to tell us: "When you prepare a sermon, don't be like the person who brings the recipe from the kitchen to the dining room table; bring the finished product when you bring the sermon in and leave the recipe in the kitchen. That is, all the research you have done on the sermon, you don't have to bring it out and display it in front of the people. Bring the finished product to the people instead." That is good advice. "If he is the Christ, tell us plainly."

Therefore I feel that it is the order of the church to repent, to speak more plainly of Christ. Let's look at the other side of the coin for just a minute as well. I would say we are to speak plainly of Christ up to a point. At times, when clarity is important, we should not and we cannot satisfy the demands for clarity or plainness. We should know. Why? Because there is a kind of clarity that the average person is asking for, which is best described by the term "computer clarity. " It's a grim point, but a good computer joke about the man who stood before the computer, a massive machine, and asked this question: "Is there a God?" And the answer came from the computer, "There is now. "

Computers are helpful when it comes to questions of fact and quantity.

But what about questions which deal with the mysteries of loyalties and the mysteries of relationships? Can we give easy answers to hard questions, and if we do, are we not succumbing to the heresy of exactness?

There are questions of the heart which can never be answered by the plainness of a T. V. commercial. The Bible, my friends, is not an almanac, nor is the preacher an answer man. We do not have all of the answers plainly to the great mysteries of life, nor can we be exact about these mysteries.

Take, for example, a tear. Let me give it to you—what is a tear? Right from the unabridged dictionary—"A tear is a drop of saline watery fluid continually secreted by the lacrimal gland between the surface of the eye and the eyelid, serving to moisten and lubricate these parts and keep them clear of foreign particles. " This is a tear?

The Saturday Review carried a question not so long ago from a very disturbed mother. The question was given to this disturbed mother by her pre-school girl. The pre-school girl had asked this mother, "Where was I when you were a little girl?" And so the Saturday Review ran it and two very interesting answers came.

The first answer came from a woman who said that she had a four year old son who asked her the same question: "Where was I when you were a little girl?" She said, "This is the answer I gave. I told my son the truth. I gave him the facts." A four year old! She said, "Half of you was a little tiny egg waiting in a very special place in my body all the time mommy was a little girl. Then when mommy grew up and became a lady, your father planted a little seed and that made your egg whole and then you grew."

The other answer came from a teaching nun. "Where was I when you were a little girl?" She said the answer is very simple; "I was in the mind of God."

I grant you that both answers have their place, but doesn't it seem to you that the second answer is truer to life because it guards the mystery. The first answer is so factual that it obscures the deeper truth. Moreover, we cannot have a gospel mix of light and mystery always explained with exactness. The gospel itself is the unveiling of a mystery, and at every stage of our Christian experience we have both meaning and mystery. We have to keep that balance. We cannot explain it all; otherwise we obscure the truth.

For instance, what does the word "obscene" mean? The word "obscene" means, "To bare that which should be hidden." In our zeal sometimes to declare the truth we should be careful that the words alone are understood as not being able to do it all, because words tend to dissipate the very mystery in which we must participate.

You take the mystery of good and evil. G. K. Chesterton wisely noted, "The troublesome thing about life is not that it is rational or irrational; the troublesome thing about life is that it is almost rational." There is always mystery.

Job, for example, grappled with this whole problem of good and evil. How can you reconcile a good God to an evil in this world? But Job was never given the answer. He all of a sudden found himself, by God's providence, in a place where the mystery no longer disturbed his faith.

An American soldier killed a German soldier head-on in World War II. He always felt that this was an unnecessary killing, since the victim was a very youthful man and this made it doubly hard for his conscience to accept. But this American soldier was given the Silver Star for his achievement. This brought additional gilt and he was distraught.

He decided that he would go to the chaplain. So the first chaplain he went to he took the Silver Star and he threw it in front of the chaplain and he said, "Justify this." The answer which the chaplain gave to him was, "Render unto Caesar what is Caesar's," then stopped. The soldier grabbed the Star and said, "To hell with Caesar," and walked out.

He went to the second chaplain, his heart burdened, and he told him the story. And the chaplain's answer was "Onward Christian Soldiers." He picked up his Star and left the second chaplain as well.

He finally went to the third chaplain who happened to be a Southern Baptist preacher. He took the Star and he threw it down and he said, "Justify this." The chaplain, upon hearing the story and seeing the distraught man broke down and cried. And all of a sudden the soldier cried with the chaplain. They wept together. Finally they prayed.

The soldier's question called, not for clarity, but for empathy. "If you are the Christ, tell us plainly." "If he is the Christ, tell us plainly."

We within the church must work to clarify our words and meaning, but we must also let the mystery stand.

Sermon preached by Dr. Vahe H. Simonian, Senior Pastor
Pasadena Presbyterian Church
April 27, 1975

Don't Send Your Children To Church, Take Them

How did I learn about the Bible? By going to Church with my folks. From a very young age I remember the Church they attended every Sunday. Once a year the Church had a revival and children age twelve and older were given the chance to join the Church. A young person growing into adulthood is responsible for his or her actions and their sins are no longer on their parents. During the revival in this Baptist Church I remember having to sit in the front row. The preacher would preach at you, to you and around you about coming to God and Jesus, accepting the Lord and walking out in God's Word. During that revival week we all joined the Church and were baptized.

What's new? I was already going to Church, Sunday School, B. V. P. U, and singing in the Choir. From time to time I would attend Bible training conferences and workshops and my various reading materials would come from there. As I was growing into adulthood, studying the Bible became part of my life and I fell in love with the great stories that I read and studied in the Bible.

I was fascinated with Jesus and I still am. Young folks in general have difficulty in attending Church, Sunday School and Christian Education classes because they are not sufficiently developed mentally to delve deeply into God's Word and understand it. I learned that Bible stories are wonderful because they point to a great morale. Each story will help you as you make a wider and deeper study of the Bible. For instance, the story of David and Jonathan will show you what a great thing true friendship is and the story of Belshazzar's Feast will show you the danger and punishment of sin.

Getting acquainted with the Bible, the Books of the Bible and the people in the Bible is not easy. It's hard and it takes a lot of study. When I learned about the three children of Israel who went into the fiery furnace I wanted to read and learn more.

When I was very young I learned that Jesus is the great objective of Bible study. The most important thing to remember, and never forget, is to learn about Jesus. If you don't learn about Jesus, all studying of the Book of Books is not worth very much.

Study the message that Jesus and John proclaim. It is our witness to the world. In Jesus I learned that we are delivered from fear to love. We don't have to threaten, intimidate, manipulate or dominate people. We are associates of the Creator and if His love flows through us we see all persons as children of the Creator and we will relate to them with grace, truth and honor. The Creator's power is the spirit living in us and His power compels us to love each other responsibly.

SCRIPTURE

In writing this book I pray for the Lord to guide me, to teach me to do His will, not mine. I don't want my stories to be contrived. I am guided by the Holy Spirit who took possession of the prophet's mind and spoke just what God wished Him to say (Peter 11: 1; 19-21).

Preachers and ministers, make your calling and election sure by being strict and obedient to all the requirements of the Gospel and by appropriating its gracious promises. Such a life will confirm both your calling and your election. Preaching is not a theatrical production with pay. Do God's will, not yours by changing His Word. No devised stories (Peter 11: 16). It is a terrible thing to fall in the hands of the Lord. Teach Jesus' teaching, His Word (Romans 1: 17; 18). No one should be surprised that sin makes God angry. God calls His preachers His servants, those who He wants to do the preaching of the Gospel (Matthew 10: 1-5) (Luke 10: 1;9). Clothing them with the power to do His work (Luke 24: 49) (Acts 1: 8) (Gal: 16). The Holy Spirit appoints every pastor over every Church/Assembly and the special work of pastors is to feed the members of His flock in   the world (Acts 20:28) (Peter 2:2). Do God's Will (James 17). Teach and preach God's Word and don't stumble over the Gospel (Peter 1: 5) (Revelations 22:18).

Those who have added to or taken away from God's Word will meet a dreadful doom as a result of their rashness. This applies to every inspired Book of the Bible. Jesus testifies that "I come quickly to call each one to give an account of his/her stewardship and to reward or punish each according to his works" (James 1:17). Teach God's Word (Peter 1:2). Foreknowledge: God always knew all that would ever occur in the world. God's election or choosing of His people for salvation was according to His foreknowledge. Accompanying that election is the sanctifying work of the Holy Spirit Who bestows a spirit of obedience in the believer who is cleansed through the blood of Jesus. God's purpose was never to save people in their sins but to save people from their sins. Don't stumble over the Gospel. Teach it.

THE ONLY POWER

I've always tried to look beyond myself. It was always I, my, and me. I knew the Lord God and His Son Jesus and enjoyed stories about the Lord at an early age. Acts 27 teaches to wait on God, don't tempt Him and put Him in a box because God is our beginning and our ending. There is and always will be the Lord God. Seek Him and live. Our Father, the creator and supreme being of this world, the creator of the universe and the only power there is and ever will be became flesh and dwelled in this world as a human being, a man. This is a great mystery.

O Lord our God, how excellent is your name in all the earth. What is man that you are mindful of him? (Psalms 8:1) (Corinthians 1:27) God chose man and man was made by God and for God. Our heritage is with God (Ephesians 1:11) (Isiah 44:2). God does not call many into His service who are considered great in this world but He chooses feeble and unpromising instruments to confound and overthrow the proud and mighty (Hebrews 4:12).

God knows our thoughts and the Word of God is living. All of His teachings, both in the law and the Gospel, are full of life, sharp and powerful in their effects (Ephesians 6:17) (Revelations 1:16;19). A dividing of soul and spirit, the Word, accompanied by the Holy Spirit, uncovers and reveals the evils of the soul and of the spirt. God is able to discern the thoughts and intents of the heart. The Word lays open the secret thoughts of the heart (Romans 7:7), Psalm 8), What is man? (Amos 4), Seek me and live (Daniel 1). Read on. (Corinthians 1:27), God chose … you did not choose me (John 15:16). Jesus first chose the disciples.

God's Word is true. I pray to let me follow You, Lord Jesus (Matthew1: 5;7). Let me be a true servant of God and discern the compassion and power that comes when one can hold the condemnation of another. It is paradoxical that "religious people" (models of public piety) are quick to judge and condemn others (Matthew 1:6;9). Do not your righteousness before men to be seen in order to gain their favor or admiration because it is an abomination in the sight of God (sin). In worship the focus must be on God (Acts17:22). It seems that God is involved in the everyday affairs of man (Mark10:18;26). Only God is good (James 1:17). Don't take God's gift for granted, Christians. One of the happiest things in my life is to be enrolled in the program of the Lord God and His Son Jesus. I worship at the Pasadena Presbyterian Church in Pasadena, California.

THE LORD GOD GAVE US HIS SON JESUS (JOHN 3:16)

In the beginning God created the Heaven and the Earth (John1:31). Study the Bible, not as the word of man but as it is truly the Word of God. Believe it. It is your choice. God created man in His own image. He created male and female (Genesis1:27) (Matthew19:4). Jesus answered the Pharisees by asking them if they did not read that He who made them from the beginning made them male and female. Oops! Did God make a mistake? I don't think so. God formed man from the dust of the earth, breathed into his nostrils the breath of life, and man became a living being (Job 33:4) (Genesis 7:22) (Corinthians 1:15;45). The Lord God said it is not good that man should be alone and He made him a helper comparable to him (Corinthians 1:11;8, 9). The Lord God caused a deep sleep to come on Adam and He took one of his ribs and made it into a woman and brought her to the man (Tim1:13) (Hebrews 13:4). Adam said, "Bone of my bones and flesh of my flesh, she shall be called woman. " Read (Matthew19:5) (Mark10:6-8). Jesus is preaching.

Marriage was instituted by God (Genesis 2:18-24) (Matthew19:5) (Cor11:8-9) (Cor. 7:2). A man shall leave his mother and father and be joined to the woman, his wife, and they shall become one flesh. A man is married to a woman and they become husband and wife.

DIALOGUE ON THE PROOF OF GOD'S EXISTENCE

It is wonderful to attend a family gathering, church, or party at someone's home where young people and college students are mixed in with adults and often get pulled aside for one thing or another. My grandson, Jonathan Williams is a Cal State Pomona student and his class was studying a book titled *Does God Exist: A Dialogue on the Proof for God's Existence* by Todd C. Moody. Jonathan was fascinated with this study topic and argument and when he came to a family gathering we talked about this book. It was interesting because Jonathan and his girlfriend Burgundy were deeply involved in sports, especially basketball, and they saw me as religious but I don't know why. These young folks place their nouns and pronouns carefully when discussing this book.

Over the years I have learned to get to know the mind of man and listen to his words. This book, or the argument "Does God exist?" got the attention of my grandson and his girlfriend and they invited me into their conversation. I listened with interest and suspense. All such discussions are unprofitable and vain (Romans 16:17;18). Read the Scripture and never be a "know-it-all" (Genesis1: 1) (John1:1). Seek (Matthew 6:33). The wisest thing to do is to learn of God, His Son Jesus and His Righteousness. All of your blessings will come to you with faith in the Lord God and His

Program. Study His Word and you will find (Matthew 6:32). Nations are seeking and the heathens are concerned about what to eat, drink and wear. Learn of God and follow Him because He does exist. If He didn't there would be no you, no us. The earth is the Lord God, the whole world belongs to God and all that is in it, including all people of one blood.

How good is it that the Lord God and His Son Jesus exist? He was not treated fairly in the things He didn't like. Do you think, if only once, He would give up and say, "That's it, I'm through, I have had enough of those people on earth so this is what I will do. I will give an order to the sun to cut off the heat supply, to the moon not to give light and to the oceans to run dry. Then, to put the pressure on and make things really tough, turn off the vital oxygen until every breath is gone." You know that He would be justified if fairness was in the game because no one has been more abused or met with more recklessness than God. Yet He carried on, supplying you and me with all the favors of His Grace for free.

People say they want a better deal so they go on strike but what a deal we have given God to whom we owe everything. People don't care who they hurt just to get the things they want. What a mess we would all be in if we all believed that God did not exist.

SIN

The Devil was smart and clever back in the time of Jesus and his influence is much worse today, especially among professional church leaders and Christians. The serpent asked the woman if God really said don't eat of every tree in the garden (Genesis 3:1-24). The woman said that we can eat the fruit of the garden but not of the fruit tree which is in the middle of the garden. God said, "Do not eat it nor shall you touch it, lest you die." The serpent told the woman, "You will not surly die." Then the Serpent began to counsel her: "God knows when you eat of it your eyes will be opened and you will be like God." Knowing about good and evil, Eve was overreached by Satan. Many of us, through faults of our own, accept Satan's devices in the world and he is leading people to hurtful extremes. As a Christian and follower of Jesus, don't be over-reached by Satan and don't be ignorant of his programs. Eve followed Satan, not God. She ate the fruit of the tree which was in the midst of the garden and fed it to Adam. He ate it with his eyes opened and his was the bigger sin. The eyes of both of them were opened and they saw that they were naked. God said, "I command you that you should not eat of the tree." Finger pointing started between Adam, Eve and God and God told the serpent, "Because you have done this you are cursed on your belly and you shall go and eat dust all the days of your life." God said to the woman, "I will greatly multiply your sorrow and conception. You shall bring forth children and your husband shall rule over you. Adam, your husband who did not listen to God is cursed to the ground for your sake. You shall eat thorns, thistles and herbs of the field all the days of your life. In the sweat of your face, out of the ground you were taken and to dust you are returned." God sent Adam from the Garden of Eden to till the ground and said to him all of the above and more, "Because you have listened to your wife and eaten from the tree that I told you not to (Sam1:15;23), cursed is the ground for your sake." (Romans 8:20-22).

MADLYN'S PERSPECTIVE

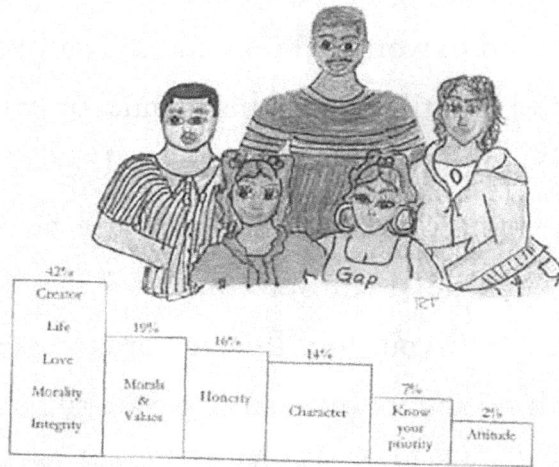

Artwork by Reana Trone

"Jesus Christ" and the Bible scriptures with humorous sketches from me, my life has always reminded me to thank God for my family and that meant to give up my seat at church today to visitors and welcome this wonderful family. Einstein once said, "You can be brilliant, but if you can't state it in a simple way, then your brilliance isn't worth much. " Everyone around the world knows what this day is highly celebrated for, "Christ has risen."

I learned early that Jesus died, was buried, and rose from the grave that we might live, if we believe in him. Whether you/we believe it or not, it is true, Christ died for our sins, that we might live and worship him only, "thou shall not have no other God before our Father, our Lord and Savior, Jesus Christ." He is our life. If he had not risen, there would be no us. The reason people are confused about their purpose in life is because they are looking in the wrong places. Society says look within and you will find your purpose. That doesn't work. Since I didn't create me and you didn't create you, we can't tell ourselves what our purpose is. We were made to know God and made for God to worship him and follow him, and him only. You will never understand it until you read his manual or pray to the inventor. I think the Bible is the ultimate owner's manual. There is always something good in your life, no matter how bad things are and vice versa. God is more interested in our "character than our comfort. " Don't let power, money and fame be the center of your life. The creator is the only power there is. We all know something about power since we are supposed to be the most powerful nation in the world. Since World War II we've been in a strong position in the world. The Atomic Energy Commission issued a statement that reveals awesome power. Man has the ability to scatter or to reduce the world to the primitive condition of the time of Cain and Abel. That is one kind of power. Prayer and faith in God is a different kind of power, the only power. In the city of Jerusalem approximately 2, 000 years ago, these two concepts of power faced each other head on in a Roman court and resulted in the drama of the cross. Pilate represented Caesar's Kingdom of Coercion and Jesus represented the Kingdom of Persuasion. Now that we have the ultimate in coercion, we should know that it accomplishes little except ultimate destruction. The message the Church has to proclaim is Christ! He is our witness to the world. In Christ we are delivered from see all persons as children of God and we relate to them with grace, truth and honor. God's power is the spirit of Christ living in us. His power compels us to love each other responsibly. Family, in all of your ways and your doings, put God, the *Creator* in our life, given to us through his son Jesus whose live is unending. He blesses us with gifts of energy, intelligence, imagination and love even though we still race after false treasures. We complain, we sacrifice our minds on the altar of ease and we are seduced by sound-byte certitudes. We shrink at the challenge of right and wrong and dress our indulgence in false hope and false words of compassion. We often turn our back on God's way. Believe me family, it is always God's will and not ours, God's way and not ours. All of us are so condescending and elite. Without the creator in our lives first, we aren't anything but a ball of dirt walking around with the creator, or Jesus Christ's life, in our body. He is our life. We see ourselves pure when we are stained and great when we are small. God is love and love must be in our heart. Love and respect for family and family members is important. Believe me, we don't have anything or own anything. It all belongs to God. Whenever we are hungry, God is there; sick, God is there with an outstretched hand. He is there for an aching heart and with family trouble he is there. Regardless of what it is, the creator is there for us but only if we trust him, believe in him and have faith in him. Love the Lord our God with all of your hearts and thou shall not have any other God before our life giver, the Creator.

Written with love in my heart for my family.

AGING

I've been in business for 47 years in the same place, growing in grace with aging.

Silly me, I never thought about aging. Nothing is going to stop you from aging physically. Society has introduced many hundreds of ways you can change your looks by doing certain things to stop you from getting older but they won't work. Our body belongs to the Creator and it is the temple where He dwells so aging isn't something that is daily on my mind. I don't get up in the morning and look in the mirror and say, "What the heck is happening?" and grab all of my stuff and put it on my face. That's what makes peace with aging for millions of people. Instead, wake up and enjoy the morning. It is a new day that you've never seen before and will never see again. Age beautifully, our body belongs to God, the Lord (Romans 8 through 11). The mind of the flesh is enmity against God, directly opposed to the Lord, and will fight Him and not submit to His rules. The Spirit of Him who raised up Jesus from the dead will make alive your mortal body and if admitted to the full control of our body, His temple (Cor. 1: 6;19). He makes you alive with the life of Jesus and He will heal, strengthen your health (Psalms 103: 3;75). Age well and be in good health (John 111: 2-7). Be in health even as your soul prospers. It is possible for one's bodily health to keep pace with that of his soul and spirit. As Jesus' life is more and more manifested in our mortal bodies (Corinthians 11: 4; 10, 11) and as our bodies receive Jesus' spirit (Roman 8: 11) we should be well, strong and vigorous regardless of age. Read the story of Moses and Caleb. Stop the false journey of aging. The Lord is in charge. Live, have faith in the Lord and look good.

IS ANYTHING WRONG ANYMORE?

Change your point of view from the freewheeling generation of today, the "anything goes" people who set their own rules. Where do our ideas of right and wrong come from? Why do we need them? Why do they change and should they change? What happens when the distinctions between right and wrong begin to lose sharpness or clarity?

A group of women club members were debating whether one of their members was right in returning a purse that she had found on a bench to its owner. They concluded that she had done a dumb thing. They decided to ask their pastor's opinion who was also a counselor. He suggested that she had done the right thing but didn't want to push his idea of right and wrong on to the women. After all, he is the pastor and counselor and doesn't he know that God is in charge? Doesn't he know that God commands us to be wise in our decisions and alert to the opportunities He provides (Ephesians 5: 15-17)? Take time out and look at several Biblical passages in which men and women had the choice of whether or not to respond to the Lord by their example, good or bad, and push His idea of right or wrong on them. What made Him think of telling people that it's wrong to steal, lie, gossip, hate, be angry, envious, jealous, hypocritical, blaming, finger-pointing and keeping evil or corrupt company (Corinthians 1:15-33)? All of the above is what the world has to offer. The Devil's Workshop creates sin and a disordered mind that makes you think you are lonely, crazy, foolish and need medication to be normal (Corinthians 2:27). Don't let the Devil and his worldly program make your mind sin and challenge you unnecessarily regarding situations, issues and conditions. The sins of fornication, uncleanliness and lasciviousness are ugly. Why was the preacher and counselor willing to concede for one second that the group might have a point when they thought the woman who found the purse was stupid to return the money? Are all of the issues above just a matter of opinion (Cor. 1:10-12)? Self-satisfaction is very perilous and full of hazards. It's time we take a long, hard look at what's happening to the difference between right and wrong; when right was right and we loved one another, family and friends, sisters and brothers in Jesus (Tim. 6: 5, 22). Don't be part of another man or woman's sins. God commands us to be careful in how we live. He teaches us to be wise in our decisions and alert to the blessings and opportunities He provides (Ephesians 5:15-17). Look at the Bible Scripture in which men and women had the choice of whether or not to respond to the Lord through good and bad examples (Mat 6:33). Seek first the wisest thing which is to get into the Kingdom of God by faith in His Son Jesus and His righteousness. The one who fully accepts Jesus and lives alone for His glory will have all the needed blessings. Worship God to get into His Kingdom by faith in His Son, Jesus. Have faith in Jesus, follow Him and live alone for His glory and you will always know right from wrong. The Gospels contain the Covenant of love and grace. God is love (John 13:34). A new commandment "Love" (Heb 7). Love is Jesus' Covenant. A man or woman who wills to obey God occupies a position taught by the Holy Spirit (John 7:17). Don't tamper with reality to make yourself look good. Stick to the facts and Jesus' teaching.

My prayer for all of you is to have healthy days ahead.

KINFOLKS

In so many ways we need to take a long look at right and wrong, love and grace, that show us how to be humble. Although we know we are somebody, it's not always about us. We all need God's wisdom. It teaches us how to think for ourselves and make decisions based on what's right rather than what's easy.

Wisdom teaches us to love God the Father and the Son Jesus, who is our life. Everything belongs to Him, "the whole realm of nature is mine", and he is a present to us, never too small! His love is so amazing, so divine and it demands my soul, my life, my all.

He is our Father from whom no secrets are hidden and we are his children of many deceptions. Lord Jesus, we say we worship you but our practices say otherwise. We allow fear to cast out love, truth is manipulated by telling lies on each other and gossip causes personal rumors and violence to fix everything. This is not God's way. God is love.

As adults we rush about filling our lives with stuff and distractions. We live double lives and that is not healthy. Oh no, no, my children that I am raising see and hear everything that I say and see all that I do.

Folks, follow Jesus. He is the way, the truth and your life. There is nothing we can do without him. Beloved, let us love one another, for love is God and everyone that loves is born of God and knows God. Let us not be Millionaire Maddocks. Always do your best to stay out of temptation (sin), and ask our Father to deliver us from evil.

Remember, I love all of you very much. Happy Holidays, enjoy the summer and don't forget to have faith in Jesus and pray. Know how to hold nothing in your heart against yourself. Jesus was not depressed, not stressed, no chemicals, no mental illness, for all of these things are of the Devil. Don't make a decision based on money but on the obedience of the Lord

Jesus' blessings. Listen to the Holy Spirit and read God's word (Scripture) and worship Jesus.

FAITH

Do you have Faith in God and His Son Jesus? When the Son of God returns to earth will he find Faith? (Luke 18: 8) Jesus speaks to some who trust in themselves, the righteous, and despised others. Please read the story of the two men who went up into the Temple to pray, a Pharisee and a Tax Collector. The Pharisee was standing, praying and bragging to God about how good he was, letting the Lord Jesus know he was great and not like everyone else, not even like this Tax Collector. The Tax Collector, standing far away from the Holy of Holies and feeling he was not worthy to approach Jesus, was hitting his breast in anguish resulting from his deep anguish over his conscious guilt and saying, "God, be merciful to me, a sinner." Repentance opens the way for genuine faith in Jesus. He forgives sins (Romans 5:1) (Hebrews 9:26)

WE MUST PRAY

We all have been born into a very sinful world, a world that is not paying attention to what God, who created this world, has said to us in His Book, the Bible. God tells us that we have all sinned and come up short of the glory of God (Romans 3:23). Everyone has turned to his or her own way (Isiah 53: 6). You see, sin is just having our own way, refusing to do God's will. The teaching of the Lord Jesus Christ is His Word. God has told us in His own words that Satan, called the Devil in the Bible, is the spirit that now works in all adults and children (Ephesians 2: 2). Satan is the opposite of God. He is the spirit of hate and all unrighteousness. Even children can tell if Satan is trying to take control of their lives. Instead of making them happy and full of love and joy as Jesus does, Satan makes them feel mean by doing mean things to others, being disobedient and wanting their own way. If Jesus had to pray, what about us and our children? Jesus' Disciples seemed unable to understand that Jesus was to be crucified. After all of His teaching, when He surrendered to His enemies they were utterly dumbfounded (Matthew 26: 54). The Disciples were soon to have their faith severely tested when Jesus went into the Garden of Gethsemane on the west side of the Mountain of Olives. The Garden is where He said His soul was sorrowful and asked the Disciples to keep watch with Him. Jesus fell on His face and prayed.

Find a quiet, secluded place so you won't be tempted to role play before God. Be as simple and honest as you can manage and the focus will shift from you to God. You will begin to sense His grace.

The world is full of so-called "prayer warriors" who are prayer ignorant (Matthew 6). Their prayers are full of formulas, programs and advice, peddling for getting what they want from God when God knows better than anyone what their needs are. A loving God loves all of us. Lord Jesus, forgive us and forgive others. Keep us safe from ourselves and the Devil. Lord Jesus, you are in charge.

Give thanks to the Lord Jesus for your life, health and strength every day; morning, evening, and night. As our lives unfold, give us the wisdom to handle every situation we encounter. Lord Jesus, let our thoughts and words be pleasing to you. I am grateful to know that where ever the mornings, evenings and nights take me, there the Lord will be. We ask the Lord Jesus to help us all to live with our mind set on the things above (Luke 18). Pray and ask the Lord Jesus to forgive us our sins.

THE EVASION OF RESPONSIBILITY (James 1:13-15)

From the beginning of time it has been man's first instinct to blame others for his own sin. The ancient writer who wrote the story of the first sin in the Garden of Eden was a first-rate psychologist with a deep knowledge of the human heart. When God challenged Adam with his sin, Adam's reply was, "The woman whom thou gavest to be with me, she gave me of the tree, and I ate." And when God challenged Eve with her action, her answer was, "The serpent beguiled me, and I ate." Adam said, "Don't blame me; blame Eve." Eve said, "Don't blame me; blame the serpent" (Genesis 3:12, 13). Man has always been an expert in evasion.

Robert Burns wrote:
Thou know'st that Thou hast formed me With passions wild and strong;
And list'ning to their witching voice Has often led me wrong.

In effect, he is saying that his conduct was as it was because God made him as he was. The blame is laid on God. So men blame their fellows, they blame their circumstances, they blame the way in which they are made, for the sin of which they are guilty. James sternly rebukes that view. To him what is responsible for sin is man's own evil desire. Sin would be helpless if there was nothing in man to which it could appeal. Desire is something which can be nourished or stifled. A man can control and even, by the grace of God, eliminate it if he deals with it at once. But he can allow his thoughts to follow certain tracks, and his steps to take him into certain places and his eyes to linger on certain things; and so foment desire. He can so hand himself over to Christ and be so engaged on good things that there is no time or place left for evil desire. It is idle hands for which Satan finds mischief to do; it is the unexercised mind and the uncommitted heart which are vulnerable. If a man encourages desire long enough, there is an inevitable consequence. *Desire becomes action.*

Further, it was the Jewish teaching that sin produced death. *The life of Adam and Eve* says that the moment Eve ate of the fruit she caught a glimpse of death. The word which James uses in verse 15, and which the authorized and the revised standard versions translate *brings forth* death, is an animal word for birth; and it means that sin *spawns* death. Mastered by desire, man becomes less than a man and sinks to the level of the brute creation.

The great value of this passage is that it urges upon man his personal responsibility for sin. No man was ever born without desire for some wrong thing. And, if a man deliberately encourages and nourishes that desire until it becomes full-grown and monstrously strong, it will inevitably issue in the action which is sin—and that is the way to death. Such a thought—and all human experience admits it to be true—must drive us to that grace of God which alone can make and keep us clean, and which is available to all.

ATTITUDE

I have love for a great high value. Cir-cum-stance, live in it but above it. The longer I live the more I realize the impact of attitude. To me it is more important than education, money, circumstances, failures, successes, what other people think, say or do. It is more important than appearance, awards, what you own, giftedness or skills.

Attitude will make or break a company, corporation, business, church, or home. The remarkable thing is that we have a choice every day regarding the attitude we will embrace for the day. We cannot change our past, we cannot change the fact that people will act in a certain way, and we cannot change the inevitable. The only thing we can do is play on the one string we have and that is our attitude.

Many years ago, as an adult I was convinced that my life belongs to me and how I react to it is what happens to me. And so it is with you. We are in charge of our attitude and we should search our heart and ask ourselves what we are thinking and if our thoughts are building us up or tearing us down (Col 3:1-8). Take control of your life and your thinking, set your mind on the things above, the Lord Jesus. It's hard to worship God or build a future if you don't get over yourself and drop your negative attitude. Circumstances can make pursuing peace and happiness very difficult. Seek the Lord Jesus and God, His righteousness, and all of His blessings will be added unto you. Don't ignore the Lord's counseling, study His word. Don't make decisions that you will later regret. Remember, from the very beginning in the Garden of Eden the Creator clearly taught that foolish decisions lead to consequences and when someone calls your attention to it you get an attitude.

THE SECRET OF WHAT IT MEANS TO BE SPIRITUAL

To find out what it means to be spiritual, perhaps we ought to visit a mental institution. That is probably the last place in the world you would think of going to learn something about spirituality. For example, in a particular mental institution, if you walked into the dining room, you would see a gentleman eating supper. He is carefully dressed; he sat down politely in his seat, unfolding his napkin, tucked it into his belt, picked up his knife and fork, and cut his meat very carefully. He changed hands with the fork, ate his peas and potatoes properly, cut more meat, dabbed his mouth with his napkin and continued for a good while. He put a little sugar in his coffee, stirred it gently, took a sip, dabbed his mouth, cut his meat.

It was something that would make Emily Post proud to watch the man. But those watching him that day noticed something very peculiar. There was no food before him, no coffee in his cup, nor sugar in the bowl. His plate was empty. A visitor said, "Excuse me, sir, but what … what are you doing?"

He looked up and said, "Why I'm going through the motions."

Folks, I think there are millions of people in the churches of America today, that are "going through the motions." There is little or no prayer in their prayers, no praise in their hymns, no attentive thought to their message, and no adoration of God. Their plates are empty, God has given us sixty-six love letters in the Bible, and in a very real sense a service of worship is a love letter to God. But such a one as I just described is no more satisfying to God than that food is to the patient.

GOD LOOKS ON THE HEART

Today we have come to offer a love letter to God. May it be one that is done from the heart in all that we do. When Judas hung himself and the disciples had the task of finding a replacement, they narrowed it down to Joseph and Matthias. Then they prayed, saying, **"Lord ... show whether of these two thou hast chosen" (Acts 1:24)**. So God looked at their faithful service, their travel with the disciples, the understanding that they had of religion and the Old Testament, and he made his decision thoroughly. No, that is not what it says. It says, **"Thou Lord, which knowest the hearts of all men, show whether of these two thou hast chosen" (Acts 1:24)**. God showed them Mathias, because he looked at his heart.

"Thou shall love the Lord thy God with all thy heart ..." (Matthew 22:37)

POOR IN SPIRIT

My continued blessings and happiness is from God's work in the world, its beauty and life. Lord Jesus, do not show a person how to be saved but rather describe the characteristics of one who has been saved. The poor in spirit are the opposite of the proud or haughty in spirit. They have been humbled by the grace of God and have acknowledged their sin and their dependence upon Jesus to save them. They will inherit the Kingdom of Heaven. The poor in spirit are happy and blessed. Those who feel their unworthiness and take a lowly place at the feet of Jesus are the opposite of the proud and self-sufficient. They have been born of the Spirit. (John 3: 3-5)

WHERE ARE THE DISCIPLES? (Revelations 21: 12; 14, 7)

Twelve (12) Gates. Twelve is a number that has much to do with God's people as the following examples show:

Twelve is the Foundation: Twelve (12) Tribes of the Old Testament and Twelve (12) Tribes of the New Testament. Twelve thousand sealed of each Tribe (chapter 7). Twelve Foundations of the New Jerusalem. On the east there are three gates and on the west there are three gates showing the city. Twelve (12) Foundations, Twelve (12) Apostles and there is one gate to each of the Twelve (12) Tribes. So there is one foundation to each of the Twelve Apostles (Ephesians 2: 20). The Walls of the City have Twelve Foundations and on them the Twelve names of the Twelve (12) Apostles of the Lamb. So where are the Twelve (12) Disciples of Jesus? Did not God choose the poor to be His Disciples? Not many wise men are called (James Interlectors 2: 5.) (Corinthians 1:21).

His Disciples, you and me, are to be enriched by His boundless grace (Matthew 21 - 45). Please read the Scripture (Jude 1 - 25). Pay attention to verse 24. God is able to keep His obedient, trusting children from stumbling over the sins of Satan and his allies that they may place in their way. To be insured of this result you must stick to God's Word and be open to the Holy Spirit's teachings. Never sin daily or have fellowship with sinful individuals. No one should be surprised that sin makes God angry (Romans 1;17, 18 and 6;12). Let not sin reign in your body or obey its desire.

REFLECTIONS ON ANGER AND VIOLENCE

I love people who are angry! I love them because I know they are alive. They feel, respond and see life as a participation event, not just a spectator sport. They have a stirring within their very soul, like a cascading stream when under control, that contains the energy to light a great nation.

I love those who act out their anger and seek to translate their discontent into a positive, moving anger that challenges those who sit by passively. I love angry people but I am concerned about people who allow their anger to explode in all directions, causing hurt in word and deed to the weak and helpless. I'm concerned about the angry, violent people who destroy both themselves and those who love them.

The world is a dangerous place. I am afraid for those who cannot talk about their anger, either because nobody is listening or their violent anger makes it impossible to communicate. Since the beginning of time, damage has been done because the energy of anger has been misdirected, turning into violence and leaving a trail of broken lives, a waste and loss never to be regained again.

The energy of anger is a *Gift from God* so there is hope for us all. It can be a source for change in ourselves and in our world. Think of the energy that anger has motivated in people who have walked out of poverty and changed their lives. Think of the athletes, writers, scholars and scientists who are making invaluable contributions to our world. Through their example and teaching, laws have been changed to bring justice and fairness into the lives of all people and this has been accomplished through the energy of anger.

I love angry people who are not content just to exist or to criticize others but I am concerned when anger becomes violent and dumps mental garbage on children and family members. I cry when I observe passiveness rather than a desire to build a positive and meaningful future for us all.

Knowing what is wrong with your life, my life, and the life of others is valuable knowledge if that knowledge creates a passion to participate in positive change. However, if that knowledge causes us to simply become accumulators of facts, critics of the culture and those within the culture, then we commit an act of indifference and stagnation.

Jesus became angry at the pompous leaders, self-righteous people who rejected the sick and the lost, and those who maintained a kind of plastic virtue. He taught that the energy of anger can be directed to produce love because He lived a life that converted the energy of anger into the power to build on love as the foundation and dynamic force in the community called Church. A community built on love not hate, inclusiveness not exclusiveness, shared righteousness not self-righteousness, building up not tearing down, redeeming and reclaiming, not just using and disposing of.

I love angry people and I hope you are angry. Turn that anger into action and open up to the spirit of God so you and all of us together can build on the foundation of love. Reject violence in all of its forms against self and others. Accept love and be a builder of self and others. First, love yourself and you will be able to love others. Keep your heart open for the Lord Jesus to dwell. He does not dwell in unclean places.

GREAT

The Government of the United States of America has always said in God I put my trust and meant it but do they mean it now? (Corinthians 1:20- 31). There is no human learning or greatness that is not found within the Gospel(Philippians 3:1). To write about the Lord Jesus is not irksome or annoying to me (Ephesians 3:1). Respect the Gospel by reading it (Hebrews 9:14). Cleanse your conscience from all the taint of sin and worship God in spirit and truth. Paul's ministry was inclusive and especially for the Gentiles. The mystery was that the Gentile believers were to be made equal in every way with the Jewish believers, remembering that the Gospel was first preached and taught to the Jews. Jesus' mission was not restricted to the Jews alone. God is the spirit of the world and we must worship Him in spirit and truth (John 1:1). Jesus is called the Word and He is the author of life and the Word of Life. Don't separate yourself from the Lord Jesus because it makes a person walk away from grace (Galatians 5). God does not allow people to trifle with Him or His requirements (Ephesians 4: 15-25). Many people don't relish spiritual things and they put themselves first (Matthew 7:6). Please read (John 1:15-18). The Law was given by Moses but grace and truth came through Jesus (Corinthians 1:4; 6). Teach what is written, the "Word" (Hebrews 10:7) that comes in a volume of books for you to read (Galatians 2:19). Don't set God aside because we need the Lord Jesus, our counselor and our advisor. Pray, have faith and believe from your heart that He answers prayers and He is One you can depend on (Matthew 6: 31-32). Our Heavenly Father knows all our needs (Acts 9: 1-9). Trust in the Lord and don't flip-flop with God's Word. Do His Will and not yours. Jesus teaches the important principle that a man who wills to obey God occupies a position to be taught by the Holy Spirit (John 7:17) (James 3: 1-18). Don't become a preacher of mere intellectual conception (Matthew 20: 28). Jesus did not come to be ministered to. We are to do God's Will (Proverbs 3:19). The Lord in His Wisdom created the earth and with His understanding He established the heavens. In seven days He rested. If you believe this God will bless you and you will live each day in thanksgiving.

MY SURROUNDINGS, MY TIME, MY PLACE, MY SELF

The Holy Spirit saith if today you hear His voice (Hebrews 1:7). The household of Jesus is Faith (Psalms 95:7-10). Today is God's time and it is always today, now. As a son, Jesus was faithful to the household of Faith. Moses was a servant in the Lord's house to testify to the truth spoken by Him. Remember that today is God's time and it is always now if we hear His voice. Jesus is the builder and proprietor of the institution of Christianity and He has accomplished this as the Son under the appointment of the Father.

Family, sisters and brothers, let us take heed so long as the time and opportunity are given to us to repent and get things right with Our Lord and Our God, the Creator of the Universe. The Word became Flesh and dwelled in this world as a man, a human being with the only power there is and the only power that will always be. This is a mystery in our world that Jesus has the authority over all flesh for the salvation of all believers (Matthew 28:18).

Jesus has authority (Hebrews 4:12) and He is able to discern your thoughts (Timothy 1:4; 13-16). Read the Scripture (John 2). Jesus is praying to His Father who is in Heaven. Pay attention to verse 9 where

He is praying for His Disciples, not for the world. Study God's Word and pray. Christians, preachers and teachers, teach God's Word and do His Will. He doesn't need our help. The Word was God and is God (Colossians 3:11). Let us put sin away and also the man-made barriers that divide people (Romans 12:2). There is no authority except from God (Titus 3:1). Remember that we were once sinners. Please read (Timothy 1:5, 6, 22). I will repeat, don't be part of another man's sin (Corinthians 6: 14-18). Unbelievers, follow the Lord God, have Faith in Him and His Son Jesus, trust Him, He will direct your path and show you the way. The Lord Jesus never wanted anyone to stumble through life. Many of us don't have Faith in God and His Son Jesus so we don't trust Him (Proverbs 3:5). Trust Him and don't lean on your own understanding that nourishes the vices of the old life. Don't let yourself be distracted by today's ceremonial, cultural and social distinctions. The Lord Jesus is what matters. Jesus is His name and Christ is His title (Matthew 32-38). Jesus is talking to His Disciples … the harvest is indeed abundant and many hundreds of millions need the Gospel. Let us pray that the Lord of the Harvest send forth laborers into His Harvest. It is God's Will to call, equip and send forth laborers into His Harvest so let us all pray, followers of the Lord Jesus, us Christians. It is important for those who attempt to preach or teach to be imbued with the power for this work (Luke 24: 49) (Acts 1:8) (Galileans 1: 16). Supreme qualifications are necessary for preaching. Preachers must receive their message and commission directly from God.

Letters From Madlyn

To My Family

🜃

It's your move, parents. Tell your children the truth, always, whether they are one or seventy-one years old. Stand together as a father and a mother, showing respect and honesty in all you say and do, when you are together and when you are not. You know that the Lord teaches us in His commandments, to honor our fathers and mothers.

Five thousand years ago Moses said: Pack your camel, pick up your shovel, mount your ass and I shall lead you to the Promised Land. Five thousand years later, Franklin D. Roosevelt said: Lay down your shovel, light up your Camel, sit on your ass, this is the Promised Land. Every president since Roosevelt has taken your camel, sold your shovel, kicked your ass and showed you there is no Promised Land.

Mother and father, teach your children the truth, not lies, not hate, evil, envy, malice or deceit. All of these are from the devil's workshop and can only lead to destruction. Mothers and fathers together, it's your move, through Jesus Christ that you have accepted Him as your Lord and Savior.

As a father pitieth his children, so the Lord pitieth those who fear Him (Psalm 103:13). Remember to tell your children:

I gave you life.
I cannot live it for you.
I can teach you things.
I cannot make you learn.
I cannot make you listen.
I cannot make you hear.
I can give you directions.
I cannot be there to lead you.
I can take you to church.
I cannot make you believe.
I can teach you right from wrong.
I cannot always decide for you.
I can tell you that you are pretty.
I cannot make you beautiful inside.
I can offer you advice.
I cannot accept it for you.
I can give you love.
I cannot force it from you.
I can teach you respect.
I cannot force you to show it.
I can teach you to obey.

I can teach you about sex.
I cannot keep you pure.
I can tell you the facts of life.
I cannot build your reputation.
I can tell you about drinking
I cannot say "No" for you.
I can warn you about drugs.
I cannot prevent you from using them.
I can tell you about lofty goals.
I cannot achieve them for you.
I can teach you kindness.
I cannot force you to be gracious.
I can warn you about sin.
I cannot make you moral.
I can love you as a son or daughter.
I cannot place you in God's family.
I can pray for you.
I cannot make you walk with God.
I can teach you about Jesus.
I cannot make Him your Savior.
I cannot make Jesus your Lord, or
tell you how to live.

MATURITY

MATURITY is to never measure wealth by money but by your life, your health and strength.

MATURITY is patience. It is the willingness to pass up immediate pleasure in favor of the long-term goals and gain.

MATURITY is plans that should be made in view of uncertainty; proper expression is if it is the Lord's Will.

MATURITY is to ask the Lord Jesus to let you be filled with the full knowledge of your will in all wisdom and spiritual understanding.

MATURITY is the ability to control anger and settle differences without violence or destruction.

MATURITY is perseverance, the ability to sweat out a project in spite of opposition and discouraging set-backs.

MATURITY is unselfishness, responding to the needs of others.

MATURITY is reading your Bible so when you attend church, you will know whether or not the preacher is preaching God's Word or his own. Study the Lord Jesus' teachings.

MATURITY is the capacity to face unpleasantness, frustration, and disappointment without becoming bitter.

MATURITY is humility. A mature person is able to say, "I was wrong." He or she is able to say, "I'm sorry" and when proven right, the mature person need not say, "I told you so."

MATURITY means dependability, integrity and keeping one's word. Don't be a gossiper and liar. Immature people have excuses for everything. They're always accusing, finger-pointing and blaming others for things they know nothing about. They are chronically tardy, no-shows and gutless wonders who fold in a crisis. Their lives are a maze of broken promises, unfinished business, former friends, and good intentions that never materialize.

MATURITY is the ability to live in peace with that which we cannot change.

Check out your "Mind." Are you **MATURE**?

YOUR

MIND

BODY

AND

SOUL

ACTUALLY

COME

WRAPPED

IN

LOVE

AS

A

GIFT

FROM

GOD

AND

HIS

SON

THE

LORD

JESUS

Notes

℘

STAY IN CHARGE OF YOUR MIND

Stay in charge of your mind and know that God created you, every little thing about you. You have special gifts to contribute to this world and a mind to carry out his mission that he planned just for you. The Lord knows you better and loves you more than anyone would or could. I am talking about our loving Father and faithful friend.

ART

Family and friends, there is a special art to living and we learn it as we grow in wisdom. It is not automatic. It is the work of the mind that concentrates on good things. It is the work of joy, tears and love. A person who wills to obey God and His Son Jesus is in a position to be taught by the Holy Spirit. Accept the Lord Jesus as your Savior. He is in charge.
(1 Corinthians 1:13) Don't keep company with sin. Choices are important. Who are you going to follow? I am, and will always follow the Lord Jesus. Family, choose the Lord Jesus and don't follow man/woman/friends. God is in charge.

DON'T LET

Don't let your mind be undermined. Don't let the Devil take over your mind. Demons and evil spirits seem to occupy many people, holding him or her as their own possession until the Lord Jesus comes and casts them out (Matthew 12:29) (Luke 11:21-22). They are agents of disease (Luke 13:16) (Acts 10:38), deafness and dumbness (Matthew 9:33-12:22). People, stay in charge of your mind. There is nothing wrong with God's world, it's the people, us, that live in the world. You know the bad, bad things going on in the world. If the Lord Jesus, the Holy Spirit, doesn't dwell in your heart, soul, mind, and conscience, you will lose your mind and the Devil will tell you what to do. Remember that Simon was endowed with supernatural power and intelligence but it was all from Satan, the Devil (Acts:8;13, 13). Today, Satan, demons have the same power. Satan is deceiving many people, capturing their mind in various bad ways. Simon believed in Jesus. He had an intellectual belief just like the demons have (James: 2; 19). Now there is no proof that Simon really repented of his sins. His mind led him to believe. Just by his name and by using sorcery he was the great one. He wanted the power that the Apostles had and he offered to buy the Holy Spirit. People in the world at every level, on every subject, answer the Devil and his demons. They rule, control and regulate your mind and you let another demon person think for you (Galatian:6;4-5). Bear your own load, your responsibilities and your own sins (Romans 1; 21 through 32). Maybe you have known God and walked away from him thinking that the world had more to offer. Follow Jesus, don't follow sinners, demons, lunatics in asylums and possessed people whose reason has been undermined. Lunatic asylums, saying you can't remember, forgetfulness, gossip, lying, diseases of all kinds and sicknesses of all kinds come to us as a result of sin and drunkenness (Luke 21:34) (Romans 13:13) (1 Corithians 5, 11, 8, 6, 10) (Galatians 5:21) (Ephesians 5:12) (1 Peter 4:3).

LOVE LIFE

Your mind, soul and body actually come wrapped in love, a gift from God. Seek first His Kingdom. The first and wisest thing to do is to get into the Kingdom of God by Faith in His Son and to be clothed in His Righteousness.

SIN

(Galatians 5:16-21). Workings of the flesh are specimens of a corrupt human nature and are manifested in uncleanness, fornication, lasciviousness, idolatry, jealousies, division, reveling, hateful strife, and murder. (Galatians 6;3)

THINK FOR YOURSELF

Your mind can go regardless of age so don't use words like "I can't remember". A very frustrated young lady called 911 on her cell phone to report that her car had been broken into. "They've stolen everything; the radio, my dashboard and compass, even the steering wheel."

MIND

The dispatcher responded, "Stay calm, a police officer is on the way." Minutes later the officer arrived and radioed in, "Disregard that last call. She got in the backseat by mistake." If you think of yourself as being something, having an exalted opinion, knowing it all, your mind and your pride cause evil. Corrupt company and all of the above cause sins for the world so let your mind tell you "no" to those things (1 John: 1 through vs. 15). Don't let your mind tell you that you are lonely. A disordered mind will tell you that you are crazy and foolish.

Love not the world and its treasures and honors (Matthew 6;19-24).
Keep in mind that your social status means nothing to the Lord Jesus.
In Him we live and move (Acts:17, vs. 28).

He is not far. In fact, the true God is in the reach of those who seek Him. The conscience of man dwells in his heart that acts as a moral regulator for what is right and wrong. Since thinking and memory are functions of the heart where God lives and communicates to us, God supplies all our needs.

See what the Bible teaches about God: He gave us His Son Jesus. He never causes what is wicked. It is unthinkable for a true God to act wickedly, for the Creator to do wrong. The Lord Jesus loves us and this is why He taught us to pray: Our Father in Heaven, let your will take place in Heaven and on Earth (Matthew 6; 9-10). And don't forget (John:3;16) God's love is great and we are to love God, love ourselves and love others. No one should be surprised that sin makes God angry (Romans 17;18).

"MIND"

Don't let the Devil leave you to believe that your problem is too much for you. Take time to know the Lord is in charge and go to the Lord Jesus for answers. Don't feel that the only option is to kill yourself and others. If you do this you are going to Hell (Matthew 12:30). Don't take your life or murder. Pain and suffering is demons and sin.

§

People in the world are full of Misery

And Shame.

Unbelief is dangerous Have Faith in God. Pray (Matthew 13:54).

We all need the Holy Spirit (Romans 8:26).

The Bible, study it.

A Nation that doesn't study history, becomes history.

I pray that you have a healthy and peaceful 2016.

Madlyn Richard (November, 2015)

§

GOD OF THE UNIVERSE IS LARGE
Big
(Romans 6: 12-23)   (Matthew 10: 40-22)

Let us not be wise in our own eyes (your eyes). Fear the Lord and depart evil, **sin** (Romans 12:16). It is wise not to let **sin** exercise dominion over your mortal body and make you obey its **desire**. Uuh, ooh, my **desire**! I can make you believe it's all about me; I, my, and me. It is easy to obey a **desire** that lacks impulse control and makes me choose to enslave myself to a society and culture that believes anything goes. I'm a grownup and I can say whatever I please no matter how rude, cutting, sarcastic, nasty, or hurtful it may be. Hey, it's a free country and if you can't deal with it, it's your problem.

Your **desire** is not power or "I am in charge." It is **sin**. Why are people so angry, mad, rude? They have a **desire** to control and can't take care of themselves but want the power to control others. Do you not know that if you present yourself to your worldly desires or the desires of others you become obedient slaves? Your **desire** of the world makes you a slave of the one you obey and being a slave to **sin** leads to death. Keep in mind that the wage of **sin** is death but the free gift of God is Eternal Life in Jesus Our Lord. (Matthew 13; 15-16)

Family, Sisters and Brothers in Jesus, and Friends that know God, we are all learning more about how to worship the Lord Jesus, how to do His will and not have other gods before Him. I know and believe that you believe in the Lord as I do. This is why it is such a joy to share my findings, learning and beliefs with you. I am humble and thankful for your response. We are all trying to do God's Will and no one is perfect but God. Be humble. This, in a sense, is done when one makes a complete surrender of his or herself to God and allows God to be Manager at His Will. Cast all of your anxiety on Him because He careth for you (Peter 1: 5-7). Take all of your troubles, burdens and problems to the Lord Jesus. Think differently and stay away from **sin** and the worries of the world around us.

Don't get involved in others sins. Have faith, pray and follow the Lord Jesus (Colossians 3:11). Put away sin, man-made barriers that divide people and vices of an old life. There are no national, ceremonial, cultural or social distinctions. The Lord Jesus is what matters. Old ways won't open new doors.

Thanks for the many phone calls, gifts and wonderful notes with Scripture for me to write about. Please give to your favorite Charity and keep your notes and wonderful Scriptures coming.

Have a Happy Spring and Summer.

Love, Madlyn Richard

Toss Your Sins Repentance

Some Christian churches have many programs. One of these churches was pious and very conservative with a 3,000 member congregation. It scheduled a Repentance Sunday to seek God's forgiveness. During a period of meditation, worshipers were asked to write down their sins on pieces of paper and put them into an urn to be burned. The Reverend Jerry Hilor was visiting and said it was a very interesting service. The next day a church member who was a State legislator asked him to pray at the Capitol and represent this high-class church because the pastor was going out of town for a hearing on a gambling charge. Reverend Hilor was asked to keep this quiet and also to keep a copy of his prayer.

So he wrote a few lines as the legislature opened on Wednesday. He bowed his head, read the prayer and handed it over to the church secretary. A news reporter asked questions later. The secretary bluntly asked, "What have you done? The church you are representing doesn't care for this prayer. Do you know that you read a prayer about sin?" Reverend Hilor jumped into a tense debate about whether some things are always right and some things are always wrong.

His prayer said:

Heavenly Father, we confess that we have ridiculed the Absolute Truth of your Word and called it moral pluralism, we have worshiped other gods and called it multiculturalism, we have endorsed perversion and called it an alternative lifestyle, we have exploited the poor and called it the lottery, we have neglected the needy and called it self-preservation, we have rewarded laziness and called it welfare.

This prayer has been read in other legislatures, causing everything from applause to jeers. Reverend Hilor said, "I thought I might get a call from an angry congressman or two but I was talking to God, not them. The whole point was to say that we all have sins that we need to repent, all of us. I did not try to aim at the right or left, or consciously try to fire both ways."

The major theme in this preacher story is that people who think that either political party is going to solve this country's real problems, are dreaming. Politicians aren't big on Absolute Truth. Reverend Hilor's agenda was to pray about the sin that he sees daily in the ministries linked to the community … that is what he was thinking about as he wrote:

We have killed our unborn and called it choice, shot abortionists and called it justifiable, neglected to discipline our children and called it self-esteem. People don't listen, don't hear, are on some type of medication and want their own way. They abuse power and call it ambition.

This is a true story and the names have been changed.

Scripture
This is my commandment,
that you love one another,
as I have loved you.

~~~~~~~~~~~~~~~ John 15:12

Happy is he, whosoever shall find no occasion of stumbling in me.*
Math. 11-6

*Stumbling in me; Who does not question my Messiahship.

James 4:5

Do you think that Scripture says in vain? (Hebrews 10:7)

Jesus comes in the Bible and it has been written He came to do God's Will.

In this corrupt system many are asking why God lets bad things happen in the world?

"Really."

God is Love. (Galatians 2:6, 20, 21) Don't set aside the grace of God.

Seek God and live.

God's judgment is just. (Jeremiah 5:3) Man's judgment is sin.

There is a time for every purpose,

and everything has its time. (Hebrews 9:27) The spirit of Wisdom and Truth opens our hearts,

our ears, broadens our minds to understand His Truth, and strengthens our will to hear His Voice and trust in His Ways.

Seek the righteousness of God, learn of Him and follow Him and His Son Jesus' teaching.

When we continue to cling to old habits that keep us from the fullness of life, when we hide from His Presence, when we ignore His Guidance and avoid His Direction, then we start blaming and pointing our fingers at why God is letting this happen.

John 1:1 He is called

The Word of Life because He is the author of all natural and spiritual life.

SOCIAL MEDIA

As Christian followers of Jesus we need to take a good look at ourselves, the Church, and the use of Social Media. Do you believe that you are a person who has no worth, no chance of being what you want to be, who you want to be, and who you want to be like on Face Book? Do you want validation from the world? We are being confronted about our belief system and challenged about subjects that are ugly and sinful. Race, culture and sex are popular topics but nothing is said about the Lord Jesus and His Program.

All lives matter, God made us all and He is our Father. (Matthew 11:25-30). Submit yourself to God's Government and learn from Him (Micah 6:8). God shows to man what is good and righteous (Amos 4:5). Seek God and live.

How are we going to learn? Read and attend Worship Service and Church. Ministers are called by God to do His Will (Corinthians 1:2-16). God is pleased with those preachers who preach the Gospel even if men reject it. Those who reject the Gospel make me sad because the Gospel is our healing. Do God's Will. God is the creator of the universe, the world. He is the Supreme Being of everything. God is the Word and the Word became flesh and dwelled in this world as a human being, a man. He is the only power there is and the only power that will always be. The Lord Jesus is the Son of the Living God and His ministry is this world. God doesn't need any help.

THE WORD
Thy Will Be Done

John 17

Matthew 6: 10

Jesus, praying to His Father, says the work you commissioned me to do on this earth is completed. I manifested your name to the men of this world; your name, your character and the attributes for which your names stands. Now the Disciples understood the truth that the Lord Jesus' mighty works were the will and the appointment of the Father. Christians, do good and do the will of His Son Jesus. Jesus was chosen and He is in charge. He called His Disciples and appointed them to do the work He chose, His Will not mine. We are to worship the Lord God, we need Him but He doesn't need us. We are to do His Will, save souls and lead one another toward the place where all that one asks in the name of Jesus is granted (John 15:16). Pray from your heart and Jesus will guide you in all truth relating to the Gospel. Jesus doesn't speak for Himself but His teaching comes from His Father and is revealed by the Spirit to the believer.

THE WORD

Friends who believe in the Lord Jesus, the world can't legislate God's "Word" but the Bible can. The Word is not for sale, don't change it, but speak the Word of God as it is in the Bible.

OBEDIENCE

Don't eat of the tree.

MORALITY

Stop, take a good look at yourself, think about whether you know right from wrong and the principles of character. Morality taught wrong is sin.

I have learned to listen. If you want to get to know the mind of a man, listen to his words. In your daily talk and fellowship with friends, family, Christians and believers, does the topic of God, Jesus, the Holy Spirit or the Bible ever come up? Or are your conversations always about worldly things such as work, jobs, news, sports, politics, partying, weather, and other ugly worldly things. We talk less about the things of God than we think, even at Church.

God Doesn't Let

Anything Bad happen to anyone.

We walked away from Him.

And

Because of people's choices they have given up God

to the desire of their hearts.

Free will enables people to kill themselves. (Romans 1:18-32)

You will find in this chapter the bad and the ugly sin.

Study God's Word, His Son Jesus'

Teaching.

Please read the wrath of God.

It reveals.

God is in charge.

Notes

About the Author

Madlyn Trone Richard was born in Florida, but spent her childhood and early adult years in Alabama, earning a Bachelor of Arts degree in General Education from Alabama A & M University and working as an elementary school teacher while marrying and raising a family of seven children. In 1964 it was time for a change. After a divorce she moved with her children to Altadena, California and earned a teaching position at Los Angeles Trade Technical College. During this period she also earned degrees from the University of Southern California's Civic Engagement Initiative and from Pasadena City College in Business Finance.

In 1969, she and her second husband, Felix Richard, went into business, opening a financial services center in Pasadena, which is still owned and operated by her family today. For the past 43 years she has been active, including serving as an elder at the Pasadena Presbyterian Church. In all things, she says, she puts herself in the hands of the Lord God.

Madlyn Richard Professional Accomplishments
PAST AND PRESENT

Bail Bondsman, licensed by the State of California, Dept. of Insurance

Notary, licensed by California Secretary of State

Tax and Business Consultant

National Association of Professional Women

National Association of Business Women Owners

Career College Association

California Bail Agents Association

American Association of University Women

American Society of Training and Development

NOW Organization

Assistance League

League of Women Voters

N. A. A. C. P.

Business woman from 1969 to present, 2016

Published one book, this will be my second as an author

Mother, grandmother, great grandmother, and I'm sure great, great, great

Most of all, I thank the Lord Jesus, the Holy Spirit that dwells in my heart

National Register's

WHO'S WHO

In Executives and Professionals

Returned 3-??-99

Ms. Madilyn Richard, Executive Director
Community Business Imprv Assn
83 E Orange Grove Blvd
Pasadena, CA   91103-3419

March 5, 1999

Dear Ms. Richard:

National Register's Who's Who in Executives and Professionals invites you for possible inclusion in the upcoming year 2000 millennium edition.

Recognition of this kind is shared by thousands of Executive Men and Women throughout the United States and Canada. National Register's Who's Who acknowledges people for their individual achievements in their specific profession. As always, the upcoming edition will be registered at the Library of Congress in Washington, D.C.

Ever since the creation of National Register's Who's Who there have never been any fees associated with individual appearance. I emphasize, do not confuse National Register's with any other imitating publications that may charge fees to be included.

Enclosed is your brief National Register's Executive Invitation, which must be returned. Should there be any errors in your above name or company name, we will correct the error immediately upon receipt of your invitation. You will be contacted shortly after we receive your invitation by telephone or by mail to complete your selection.

Congratulations and Good Luck on your appearance in National Register's Who's Who in Executives and Professionals.

Respectfully Yours,

Richard S. Lloyd
Chairman

RSL:mdm

Ms. Richard, due to our tight selection schedule, a prompt response would be appreciated.

National Register's WHO'S WHO In Executives and Professionals
400 West Main Street, Suite 230 • Babylon, NY 11702
Telephone (516) 321-0007 • Fax (516) 321-0034

National Register's
WHO'S WHO
In Executives and Professionals

400 West Main St. Ste 250
Babylon, NY 11702
Tel: (516) 321-0007
Fax: (516) 321-0034

NATIONAL REGISTER'S
WHO'S WHO
IN EXECUTIVES AND PROFESSIONALS

FOR IMMEDIATE RELEASE

NATIONAL REGISTER'S WHO'S WHO IN EXECUTIVES & PROFESSIONALS
INCLUDES MADLYN A. RICHARD, EXECUTIVE DIRECTOR OF ADMINISTRATION
AT COMMUNITY BUSINESS IMPROVEMENT ASSOCIATION IN ITS
MILLENNIUM EDITION

NATIONAL REGISTER'S WHO'S WHO IN EXECUTIVES AND PROFESSIONALS has
included the individual named above for appearance in the 2000 edition.

NATIONAL REGISTER'S WHO'S WHO wishes to extend its personal congratulations to the
professional named above. The intent of NATIONAL REGISTER'S WHO'S WHO is to
notify all who read this announcement that the individual named above has reached a level of
recognizable success in their respective field.

The 2000 Edition of NATIONAL REGISTER'S WHO'S WHO IN EXECUTIVES &
PROFESSIONALS is received only by the included members. This year's edition will, of course,
be registered at the Library of Congress in Washington, D.C. .

****

CALIFORNIA
DEPARTMENT
OF
EDUCATION

721 Capitol Mall
P.O. Box 944272
Sacramento, CA
94244-2720

DELAINE EASTIN
State Superintendent of Public Instruction

March 27, 1996

Madlyn Richards, Authorized Representative
Nu-Ed Food Program (CBIA, Inc.)
(Child Care Food Program)
83 East Orange Grove Boulevard, Suite 3
Pasadena, California   91103-341983

County & Agreement:
19 1957-9M

Vendor:
B756-00

Dear Ms. Richards:

I am pleased to announce that your agency has been selected to receive the Certificate of Recognition from the California Department of Education for operating an outstanding child nutrition program.

Sponsors were nominated to receive this award based on the results of on-site reviews conducted by our field services unit staff. Your organization has demonstrated excellence in program administration, and innovative techniques in meal preparation and planning. In addition, your efforts to meet the nutritional needs of children above and beyond program regulatory requirements serve as a model for other child nutrition programs to follow. You are providing a sound foundation for children by promoting healthy eating habits and a healthy lifestyle as integral components of their educational experience. Your efforts will provide lifelong benefits to the children of California, and to our society at large.

Staff from the Child Nutrition and Food Distribution Division will contact you soon regarding the presentation of this award. If you have any questions, please contact Karen Brazille at (916) 323-1187.

Congratulations on a job well done.

Sincerely,

DELAINE EASTIN
State Superintendent of Public Instruction

DE:kb

University of Wisconsin-Stout

Menomonie, Wisconsin 54751-0790

September 25, 1996

MADLYN RICHARD
CBIA, INC NU-ED FOOD PROGRAM
83 EAST ORANGE GROVE BLVD
PASADENA CA 91103

Dear Madlyn:

It is my pleasure to invite you to travel with me on an early childhood education tour to Ireland with an extension to London, June 8-20, 1997.

This innovative educational activity focuses on a subject of interest to everyone who shares a concern for early childhood education. It also offers an opportunity to share the experience with others who have the same dedication.

The historical background and social setting of the European system has been studied frequently by educators worldwide. This is your chance to do the same. Through visits to early childhood programs, you will enlarge your understanding and appreciation of current thinking among European early childhood educators and observe the strategies being used in kindergartens, the primary grades and preschool settings. This will be a unique opportunity to see facilities, children, programs and professionals at work.

So that our trip won't be "all work and no play", we will have a very full program, including guided sightseeing tours. Additionally, you may want to plan an excursion into the lovely Irish countryside or visit nearby cities on a day reserved for independent activities. Theaters, concert halls, museums, and shopping offer further cultural opportunities that you will enjoy.

Consider participating in this many-faceted travel program with a group of people who share a common interest. Study the enclosed brochure and if you need further information, please feel free to contact me.

Phone: (715) 232-1405
FAX: (715) 232-2366
E-Mail: IN%"HERRJU@UWSTOUT.EDU"

Sincerely,

Judy Herr, Ph.D., Associate Dean
College of Human Development
Room HE 216
University of Wisconsin-Stout
Menomonie WI 54751

Attachment

To all of our clients, friends and associates:
It has been a pleasure serving you, and yours.

"The eternal God is thy refuge, and underneath are the everlasting arms..."
Deuteronomy 33:27

During our 40 years in business, our aim has been to serve people, knowing that above us is the Lord's covering, beneath us his strength and security, and around us always his arms of love. Through the spectrum of services we have offered, whether bail bonds, counseling, notary, personal and business income taxes, business start-ups and incorporation, selling and buying real estate, accounting and other profit and non-profit financial services, it has been our privilege to serve those on the bottom rung of the ladder as well as those at the top. Whether poor and homeless, materially prosperous or intellectually elite, all have been served with respect.

We learned early in our business life to work with all people. If you know us, you know that we do not tolerate racism or those who look for it. As business folks, we appeal to human pride, seeing ourselves and others as compassionate and secure, with no need for fearfulness or intimidation. We have always believed that any action in business that harms or shames another human being, even though it may further our own interests, is wrong and not to be condoned, either in the United States or anywhere else in the world.

The nicest part of writing this letter is remembering special people like you. We wish you all the old-fashioned joys of the season and bright new hopes for the coming year.

Felix Richard, Jr.
President

Madlyn Richard
Chief Financial Officer

www.ingramcontent.com/pod-product-compliance
Lightning Source LLC
Chambersburg PA
CBHW081155090426
42736CB00017B/3333